JOURNEY WITH GRIEF

Navigating the First Year

LARRY WARNER

barefooted *publishing*
Oceanside, CA 92054

Cover Design: Christine Smith
Image: Christine Smith
Interior Design: Debbi Stocco

Library of Congress Cataloging-in-Publication Data
Names: Warner, Larry, 1955- author
Title: Journey with Grief: Navigating the First Year
Description: Oceanside: barefooted publishing, 2018
Identifers: LCCN 2018907384 (print) ISBN 9780998218601 (paper)
LC records available at http//lccn.lov.gov/ 2018907384

ISBN 978-0-9982186-0-1 (print)
ISBN 978-0-9982186-2-5 (ebook)

This book is written in memory of my son, Nathan Joel Warner, whom I had the joy, and at times the anguish, of parenting for a little over 18 years. He was a headstrong individual with dogged determination and a unique way of seeing the world; he never ceased to astound me. I am grateful for the time I had with him, continue to miss him, and am still sad that I never had the opportunity to see and experience the man he would have one day become.

TABLE OF CONTENTS

Section One
For You Who Are Suffering Loss

Section Two
For You Who Journey with Others

Preface

This book was birthed in the weeks and months following the death of my son, Nathan. He died on October 31, 2003 at age 18. As I was grieving my son's death, I began to write poetry to help me process my experience. I was encouraged by friends to consider weaving the poems into a book, but at a time when my loss was still painfully fresh, I was too raw, too vulnerable. A few years later I posted some of the poems on my website (b-ing.org) under the title, *My Journey with Grief*, and have been thanked many times in subsequent years for my unedited honesty. Those emails from fellow grievers were and are wonderful gifts to me—reminders that God can and does bring good out of the horrific circumstances of life. But a book on grief never occurred to me.

In fact, the writing of this book at this time comes as a complete and utter surprise! I had been working on another project, reading and researching for over a year. I was finally getting to the writing stage when a poem about the fourteenth anniversary of my son's death welled up within me. I wrote it, *The Door Bell Rings* (see below), and posted it on Facebook. It was the process of writing that poem, and feeling the desire, freedom and willingness to post it on Facebook, that God used to show me that the wounds of fourteen years were continuing to heal, and that the twelve-year-old invitation to write about grief was now being extended by God. I immediately shelved my research, retrieved my journals from 2003–4 and changed my course.

I write this book with the hope that it will give you permission to grieve freely, openly and with unedited honesty; that it will provide valuable information to help you navigate the first year following the loss of your loved one. I pray it will assure you that you aren't crazy, that you are not alone, that there is a future and a hope for you, and finally that it will provide a sorely needed resource for others who are invited to weep alongside you. Sadly, my wife and I continue to bear the lasting pain that was inflicted by well-meaning but misguided individuals seeking to bring comfort. Comforting a grieving person is a skill, and this book will help you learn how to do it.

The first year following the loss of a loved one can be extremely difficult and my prayer is that God will use this book to help you navigate through it with insight and understanding about your experience. Each grief journey is unique; if you are single, you are naturally more alone, while if you are married, the loss of a loved one, especially a child, can be a challenge to your marriage. In this first year, your pain at times will be unbearable, but God is with you—in the darkest hour there is hope. You may not be able to hear it or believe it right now, but know this: I am believing it for you as I stand with you in your grief.

Below is the poem God used to lead me to write this book.

The Door Bell Rings

Two weeks of years
have come and gone
yet the horrifying news of that night—
remains horrific,
for time does not heal
all wounds.

Tonight I catch a glimpse
of the sorrow in her eyes
she is thinking of him
            missing him
I pause at his picture
            sighing
            feeling the pang within

time once plodding,
weighted down by our grief,
has picked up speed—
the anniversary of his
death has arrived

there is no escaping it
for tonight
as in the preceding thirteen years
the doorbell will ring
and ring and ring,

and each time we will

open the door—
to costumed children
with expectant faces
bags held in outstretched hands
reciting a sing-song chorus of
trick or treat

we too, wear a mask—
a smiling face
hiding sad eyes
as we dole out
the treats

this yearly reminder of the
horrific trick
death played on us
that Halloween
two weeks of years before

the doorbell rings—
walking to the door
we check our masks
knowing time does not heal
all wounds.

Two Introductions

This little book is intended for two separate sojourners, companions on the same journey of grief. Thus, two introductions; the first is for the person in the early stages of grief. If this is your experience, I want you to know I am sorry for your loss and hope my words will help you navigate this first year. My intention is to be practical and informative, to help you enter into and be prepared for what often takes place in the first year following the loss of a loved one.

The second introduction is intended for those invited into the grief process as sources of support to the grieving person. This is an often daunting and demanding role, yet it is hugely beneficial to those who weep. This second section is designed to help you be a life-giving, loving and healing presence in the lives of those who are grieving, rather than a source of additional pain.

Section One—For You Who Are Suffering Loss

The book you are holding is deeply personal, the product of my own grief over the loss of my son, Nathan Warner, on October 31, 2003. It also reflects my journeys over the years with many others who have suffered the gut-wrenching reality of loss. I have accompanied others as a pastor, deputy sheriff, hospice chaplain, spiritual director, friend, father, husband and son. Through these experiences I have learned that grief is highly personal, a journey uniquely plodded, offering no precise path or timetable, no right or wrong turns. This journey is also universal, a route that can be anticipated and planned for. The uniqueness and the universality exist in tension; they are both true. Reading this or any book will not take away your pain, but it may help you process and prepare.

Grief isn't something to overcome, although it's natural to wish it away.

Grief is normal. It doesn't demonstrate an absence of faith or trust in God (Jesus grieved). Rather, one's willingness to enter into and embrace grief honestly is a declaration of faith and trust in God, especially when God's presence may feel painfully lacking. Grieving helps us to name and process loss, to begin to be open to a new normal. There is no time frame, but a new normal does come into existence over time. And there is no truth to time healing all wounds; only eternity heals all wounds.

This first section is specifically written for those who have been recently stung by death. I have included some of the poems I wrote in the days, weeks and months following my son's death nearly fifteen years ago. In addition, I include what I consider to be helpful information for navigating the first year—the first year of birthdays, holidays and anniversaries, all of which can be devastating— along with many other practical, down-to-earth insights. I hope you will feel my hand holding yours, my experience supporting and preparing you, reminding you that you are not alone.

SECTION TWO—FOR YOU WHO JOURNEY WITH OTHERS

A caring, loving person can be a powerful presence during a grief journey. If you are that person, chosen to walk with someone in the throes of loss, I congratulate you for doing all you can to prepare for this most sacred of journeys. Having said that, I caution you to not take this God-given invitation lightly—more often than not, it's a natural result of an already proven relationship, but a relationship that will never again be the same.

The first few chapters of Section Two will help you discern your role before you get significantly involved in another's journey with grief. You need to determine if you are able to be a safe haven or, if not, what you can do to support and love from a distance. Let me assure you that both kinds of care—the intimate and the distant—are enormously valuable and necessary. The more distant, practical ministry of serving enables others to focus on the emotional ministry of pres-ence, comforted by the knowledge that practical needs are being met.

In addition, you will find useful information about what to say and what not to say, the characteristics of a good comforter and the benefits and means of long-term support. You will be advised to count the cost to yourself and your faith, to be aware of the grief that will overwhelm you again and again. The truths of scripture and the promises of God will enable you to endure the wind and waves of grief—yours and your companion's—within God's gracious embrace.

Note: This book flows out of my own story, so in both sections I speak of the importance of being aware of and caring for "remaining children" without acknowledging this is not the reality of every situation. There will be some of you reading this who have lost your only child, or who have one remaining child. I am sorry for your loss and do hope that this wording does not cause you additional pain.

SECTION ONE

FOR YOU WHO ARE SUFFERING LOSS

I can offer no words that will help you speed through or detour around your grief, but I hope that by sharing in my experience, you will begin to enter into, and even embrace, your unique journey in your own way.

What follows are short chapters—almost snippets—concerning a variety of issues, events and emotions you may encounter during the first year. This is by no means an exhaustive list, but hopefully it will help you create space and foster reflection, and be more prepared to normalize what you are experiencing. I pray that by sharing my journey, I can contribute to what God is already doing in your life and move you to be open to God's presence and love even in these most painful circumstances.

CHAPTER ONE

GRIEF CHEAT SHEET—THE SHORT LIST FOR THOSE NOT READY FOR MORE

If you have no energy or desire to dig deeper into your experience, I encourage you to at least read through the bullets below. I wish I had known some of these truths as I questioned my sanity after losing our son.

- Your life/world has utterly and unalterably changed.
- Grief is natural and a necessary response to loss—Jesus grieved.
- Grief is unique, and has no precise time frame or linear path. Grief can be a very difficult road of indeterminate length, but the worst of it is often the first two to three months (even up to six months). Somewhere in that two to six month time frame, things begin to shift internally. The shifting continues as you make your way through the first year, opening to and processing what you are feeling with God and others.
- Grieve as you can, not as you cannot (be true to your process).
- Your feelings may take you toward God (life/healing) or away from God (death/destruction). The decision is yours.
- Grieving well requires you to be open and honest with yourself, God and others whom you trust.
- You have "grief brain"—your brain isn't functioning well. As a general rule, do not make major decisions for a year.
- Grief tends to isolate, but try not to cut yourself off from others.
- Not everyone is safe, so maintain good boundaries.
- The uniqueness of grief can cause difficulties in marriages and families.
- Think through, plan ahead and, if possible, talk through with others how you wish to handle holidays and annual family celebrations, including the anniversary of the death (give yourself grace; that day may be harder than you anticipate).

- Grief ebbs and flows in ocean-like waves. Rogue waves will appear out of nowhere. You may be surprised at what triggers your feelings. When an unexpected rogue wave occurs, enter into the experience as you are able, and let it take you to God. Grief is a shape-shifter!

- Make it a point to eat well, exercise and get the sleep you need.

- Even when you will not or cannot pray, the Holy Spirit is praying on your behalf, communicating your unarticulated groans and sighs to God.

- Grieving is a pathway to caring, grace and compassion for others.

- Grief is an invitation to know and experience God, yourself and others in new and deeper ways.

- You are not alone. God and others are with you.

- The loss of your loved one is not the final word—God's love and grace will carry you through. There is hope.

- God is bigger than your circumstances even if God currently feels absent.

- The overwhelming odds are with you making it through all this and even growing from it.

✈ Creating a List

The following two common and well-meaning statements are not as helpful as they are meant to be:

- "Let me know what I can do for you."
- "If you need anything, please let me know."

Because you often don't know or can't articulate what you want (grief brain) or need, or, when you do have a need, you lack the energy to contact someone, the offer goes unheeded. Often too, you have no recollection of who made the offer when a genuine need arises.

I suggest, possibly with the help of a friend, that you create a list of things you might need and keep it handy. If the list is on your phone, desk or computer, you can easily share it with a caring person who really would like to be of help.

Here are some suggestions for your list, to get you started: Do laundry, pick up children, clean house, get groceries or fresh produce, walk the dog, babysit, water plants, wash the car, write thank-you notes, respond to texts or emails, take you to get a haircut, go for coffee…

Chapter Two

My Experience

Friday 4:27 p.m.

The call came.
My son Ricky
barely understandable,
"Come home Nathan is dead."

"Okay."

Hanging up, I crumbled,
heartache and despair overwhelmed,
yet
disbelief held out false hope.

Driving toward home
streaming tears clouding my vision
sobs racking my body.

I found
my wife weeping uncontrollably,
my son sobbing.

Oh God, it's true!
Nathan is dead.
My son is gone.

I will never see him
touch him
hear him

be with him again.

Devastated, we held each other,
instinctively knowing this was but the beginning
of our long journey with grief.

This is how my journey with grief began, and in some ways, continues today. I still miss Nathan; I still wonder about the man he would have become—the uncle, father, husband. He died on October 31, 2003. He was 18 and had adventured off to college six weeks before. We had seen him the Monday prior to his death when he returned to survey the damage done by devastating fires in our area. Covered in soot, he stopped by the house with a couple of his friends to hose off. They had sneaked into the cordoned-off area to check on homes of others in their group. My wife called out as he and his friends were leaving, "I love you!"—her final words to him.

I do not remember much from the evening we received the news—the call from my younger son; the drive home; the gathering of his siblings, Stephanie, Mickey and Ricky; four friends dropping by and spending the evening with us; numerous phone calls. The desire to escape, wake up, go back in time was pervasive, along with the palpable pain that settled on each of us for a very long time. I do not remember much of that night, other than the neighbor's continually ringing doorbell and children screaming, "Trick or treat!"

Nathan was due to come home that night. Halloween was his favorite holiday. Although he wasn't a fan of candy, he loved collecting it and continued trick-or-treating through his senior year in High School—his record candy haul was over 30 pounds! This Halloween night he did not make it home from college, as his life ended when a semi-truck smashed into him early that morning.

Two days later, on a Sunday, we traveled in two cars to collect Nathan's belongings from his college dorm. It had been six weeks since we had made the initial trip, one marked by his high excitement. He had desired to go away to college his whole life, and now both his life and the adventure were over. It was surreal to pack up all that we dropped off only a few weeks earlier—all but Nathan. We met some of the friends he made, many of whom we would see again at his memorial service. We loaded the car and drove to my parents' house to tell them the news in person. It was an excruciatingly painful day.

The memorial service was held eight days later; that entire week is a blur. I remember family arriving, meals being brought in, Donna's sister, Diana, as gatekeeper against an overwhelming crush of people. I remember Cynthia helping with the video from our assembled photos, choosing the music; someone securing the church, arranging for food, getting the word out. I remember uncontrollable weeping, unbelievable pain, waking up each night at the time he died, Nathan-centered dreams, the inability to look at pictures without bursting into tears.

I remember being surrounded by family and friends that week before the memorial service. Then, like funeral flowers, they all faded away, moving on with their lives and tending to their own families. Our experience of grief, however, was intensifying, now that the preparations and hubbub were over. The distractions behind us, we—family of five, husband and wife—were left to begin in earnest our journey with grief.

Untitled

All-encompassing sadness
is my constant companion

tears
grief
sorrow
journey with me

questions
images
loss
invade my thoughts
day and night

My family will never be the same
My life will never be the same
I will never be the same

"Death, where is your sting?"
a question I never ask

CHAPTER THREE

THE JOURNEY

Walk Don't Run

lingering in the
heartache of sorrow
embracing the
devastation of grief
savoring the
ache of despair

birthing the
person of Jesus

You have lived a life-changing trauma and are holistically injured. Unfortunately, on the outside you appear to be almost the same, like someone with a back or neck injury, or one who suffers from chronic fatigue. Yet the truth is you are permanently, deeply damaged, and you need to live into that truth, give yourself grace and patience. The extent of your injury is a combination of many factors: your personality, disposition, prior mental state, image of God; the status of your relationship with person who died; your last exchanges with that person; the circumstances of the death. The list is endless, and each factor has multiple levels, all an apt reminder of the singularity of grief. Whatever the level of your pain, your life has been forever altered. There is no returning to reality as it was; the only decision ahead is to remain stuck in your pain or to move on. This choice will be eased into over the coming months, but for now, seek to own and even embrace the tectonic shift that has rocked your heart and life.

Grief is a normal, natural and necessary response to the death of a loved one. Your grief journey is to be entered into rather than aborted or suppressed. It's not something you rush through, as it will have a flow and time frame of its own—

one unique to you. If you attempt to abort, suppress or rush through the grief process, it will only fester within and seep through at a later time in unknown, unhealthy and often hurtful ways. For a time, one must abide in grief.

In many ways grief is a declaration of the love we feel for the person who is gone. It's often immediate and unstoppable—erupting from within with amazing force and power. Such was my experience at the death of my son. But sometimes it isn't as explosive—it can be more of a muted sadness, as I experienced with the death of my dad. That very real sensation of grief couldn't be trivialized, but it didn't approach the anguish I felt with the loss of Nathan. Grief follows death as winter follows autumn and is as uniquely endured.

The Power of Death

Death set Nathan apart,
transformed him,
took him.

Once he was one of four
unique,
but one of a greater number.

Now he stands alone
receives special consideration
invades my thoughts

not because of love,
because of death.

He is forever distinct
because he is dead.

Death set Nathan apart.

Death isolated him

from his brothers
from his sister
from his mother
from me.

Death defines us
now.

CHAPTER FOUR

STARTING THE JOURNEY

Moving On

there is no going back
there is no getting over it

there is only moving on
    forever changed
    forever wounded
moving on
    with pain
    with sadness
moving on
accepting the reality
of a new normal
shaped by my worst nightmare
having come true

This journey asks two things of you—openness and honesty: openness to God and to yourself, your feelings and experiences; honesty with yourself, with God and with trusted others. The grief journey will lead you either toward God (life/healing) or away from God (death/destruction). Be honest with yourself as you receptively and graciously explore your feelings and your direction. The choice of destination is yours—a choice you may feel like you are not fully able to make at this time. Please extend grace and patience to yourself while owning that a desire to desire to make a choice is an important starting point.

Jerry Sittser wrote of his grief following the loss of his mother, wife and young daughter in a car accident, "I chose to turn toward the pain...Giving myself to grief proved to be hard as well as necessary. It happened in both spontaneous and intentional ways."[1] He tells of making a choice, the same ongoing choice you will need to make, maybe not every day, but repeatedly as circumstances present themselves. It just happens; there is an uncontrollable, spontaneous reality to grief.

I liken the experience of grief to ocean waves, sometimes placid or rhythmic, and then unexpectedly crashing onto shore with power and unpredictability. The coast along the Olympic Peninsula in Washington is strewn with large tree trunks and populated with signs on tall metal poles reading, "Watch for Rogue Waves." The signs warn that out of the blue or grey, a wave can suddenly appear, possibly carrying one of these massive tree trunks, smashing onto the shore and into you.

So it is with grief. You may be driving, walking down the street, picking up something from the store, and suddenly, whack—you are flattened by a rogue wave of grief. I remember walking through the grocery store shortly after Thanksgiving, just beginning to venture out into the real world of random people, when I caught sight of a carton of premium eggnog and lost it. I wouldn't necessarily have associated Nathan and eggnog, but the rogue wave took me down. Some time later I recalled that Nathan would occasionally ask for eggnog and that he always added the reminder, "And don't get the cheap stuff." That was the latent association that prompted the wave of grief.

The process of grieving is intentional, but not forced. The intentionality is more about fostering and maintaining an inner stance of interaction with the grief process as it emerges and as you are able to in the moment. Resist the temptation to adjust your expression to the expectation of others. Grieving is not a linear, straightforward undertaking. Grieving helps you to name, embrace and process your loss, which then allows you to begin to accept the new normal: life after loss. Grief is not something to overcome, deny or move through as quickly as possible, but an avenue to healing.

Finally, there is no time frame for grief or for returning to "normal." The process is messy and unique to each individual; as it unfolds, you will gradually begin to piece together a new normal. Although you can't expect complete healing, as only eternity heals all wounds, meaningful life does exist after the death of a loved one.

If you choose to enter your journey with grief openly, and I hope you will, God will use you in the lives of others in unimaginable ways. I am not saying your experience is or will be worth the cost, but I do want you to know it will not be

---

1. Sittser, page 42.

wasted. God often uses suffering to transform individuals by inserting love and power for good into situations and circumstances that are anything but. Paul tells us in 2 Corinthians 1:4 that we are able to comfort others with the comfort we have received. Your journey will prepare you to come alongside others with firsthand knowledge of pain, love, grace and God, exceptionally equipped to live and share differently.

If you asked me, I would trade in a heartbeat all the experiences of comfort that have flowed from my journey with grief. But if your question is, have I seen God use the tragic death of my son in my own life and in the lives of others, I would immediately answer yes, in ways I never dreamed possible. Suffering is a byproduct of living in a broken world; God uses even the loss of a loved one for good.

Second Thoughts

God, did you ever have a moment of pause
*   as your Son*
*   suffered at the hands of others?*

Did you ever have a second thought (even briefly)
*   as you watched him tormented*
*   and mangled?*
Did a doubt ever cross your mind
*   as your only Son*
*   cried out in anguish?*
Did you ever have even the tiniest urge to intervene?
Did you feel anything as you watched your Son
*   brutalized?*

What about my son?

Did you ever have a moment of pause?
A second thought
the tiniest urge to intervene
*   as that truck barreled down the highway*
*   toward him?*
Did you feel anything as my son, your child
*   was pulverized*
*   and mangled by blunt force trauma?*

You Have Permission to NOT:

Answer your phone.

Listen to voice mails.

Return calls.

Respond to texts.

Have your ringer on.

Check email.

Respond to email.

Read every card.

Write thank-you notes.

Answer the door.

Accept invitations.

Respond to everyone who reaches out to you.

Open your home.

Share your heart.

Carry on a conversation.

Attend church.

Attend small group.

Allow everyone access.

Apologize for tears.

Pray (Jesus and the Holy Spirit are praying for you).

Look presentable.

Prepare an evening meal.

Maintain a spotless home.

You Have Permission to:

Ask for help with any of the above.

CHAPTER FIVE

GRIEVING ROADBLOCKS

As I previously stated, there is a choice attached to the grieving process: to enter in. Not in order to get through it, but to honestly open to your feelings and experiences. This prospect may understandably cause a twinge of resistance (maybe more than a twinge), and an uneasiness about the path ahead. If you've already committed to the journey, you can skip this chapter, but if this reluctance is even mildly present, please consider the following list of possible characteristics that may apply to you—reasons you may be reluctant to really experience your grief:

- Upbringing—having be taught to ignore or hide negative feelings, to focus on the positive, to be happy
- Unhealthy view of emotions—a view that says there's no place for anger or other negative emotions (especially regarding God)
- Fear of losing control of one's emotional self
- Fear of pain
- Misunderstanding about what God desires from and for us
- Expectations of others
- Lack of support from church community
- Fear of where grief will lead
- Desire to be a "good" Christian witness

I am choosing not to comment as to why the above reasons are invalid, but instead I want to advocate biblically for grieving. Simply, Jesus grieved. Jesus wept. Jesus felt sorrow, anger, worry (or concern) to the point of sweating drops of blood. Jesus asked why God had forsaken him on the cross, and was able to cry out to his Father in honest agony. Yes, the example set by Jesus is the most persuasive argument for Christian grieving (further addressed on pages 42-43 and pages 124–125 in Section Two). So please enter into grief, allowing yourself to experience and express what you are feeling, assured God is with you, and that grace, love and hope are present.

Before moving on, I do want to debunk the last point in the list above. The idea that grieving is the antithesis to "good" Christian witness may sound reasonable at first, but it is painfully false. If anyone is able to endure an extraordinary loss (as you have) and act as if everything is fine, it indicates an inability to face reality, a desire to escape. On the other hand, if one who has suffered an extraordinary loss is struggling, asking soul-searching questions, and somehow managing to look toward God in the midst of anger, sorrow and despair, then such faith has some substance to it. This person is an example of genuine Christian witness.

I implore you to be real, to be open, to not hide your grief from others or from God. Turn to God with all you are feeling, all you are dealing with—your questions, your anger, your pain. Your honesty invites those around you to be honest. Your grief is a both declaration of love for the person you have lost, and also of faith in the presence of God. Felt or not, God is with you. "I believe; help me in my unbelief."[2]

Isaiah 40:31

God, help me appreciate the strength you have given me.
Allow others to see it as a sign of your faithfulness.
For it is not the showy "mount up with wings like eagles"
    kind of strength
nor is it the practical, "run and not be weary"
    kind of strength.
nor is it the "get out of bed each morning"
    kind of strength.

It is the "I don't know how I'm going to make it
through the next hour minute second"
    kind of strength.

God help me prize this particular strength
and not bemoan my weakness
or my limitations,
    for at times it feels like no strength at all.

---

2. Paraphrase of Mark 9:24b.

Traps to avoid:

Pressure to grieve "appropriately"

Too loose boundaries (letting everyone have access—e.g., accepting all phone calls, all visits…)

Too strict boundaries (isolating self—excluding all others)

Going it alone

Denial of limitations

Giving friends unlimited phone access to you

Giving into pressure to be a "good" Christian/good witness

Dishonesty with God

Dishonesty with self

Denying "grief brain"

Refusing help

Suppressing your feelings

Unhealthy coping, numbing choices

Caring for others (focused on comforting/serving those who come to comfort, support you)

Not allowing others to care for you (letting people in, but not letting them care for you, serve you)

Equating moving on to a betrayal of the one who died/lack of love

Ignoring poor sleeping and eating habits

A growing distance between you and your spouse

Pressure to move on to quickly

Failure to process your grief

CHAPTER SIX

UNIQUENESS OF GRIEF

Although some characteristics of grief are universal, at least to a degree, this book flows from my experience of the unexpected loss of my son and is unique to my individual circumstances and to me. Since your journey with grief is uniquely yours, please don't compare our experiences or the magnitude of loss. It can't be done.

If death followed a battle with cancer, dementia, or some other debilitating illness, you may experience a mix of emotions, perhaps even relief. If the person who died hurt you or there were serious issues in your relationship, your experience will reflect those emotions. If the person who died always made holidays miserable, you may experience a sense of joy and freedom on those days. The circumstances of death, prior involvement with the person who died, individual personality and temperament and numerous other factors contribute to the uniqueness of each person's grief. Siblings who have lost a parent or another sibling may be able to comfort each other, but will not share the precise pace or process of grief. Spouses will experience the loss of a child differently.

No one can fully understand or enter into your individual framework. In his book *Heartbroken*, Gary Roe observes, "People may be able to sympathize and walk alongside you, but no human can fully understand your grief. It is special, and it's yours alone."[3] Wolterstorff echoes this sentiment: "Each person's suffering has its own quality. No outsider can fully enter it."[4] In *Broken Hallelujahs*, Beth Slevcove advises "…my best advice on grief: grieve as you can, not as you can't."[5]

---

3. Roe, page 129.
4. Wolterstorff, page 72.
5. Slevcove, page 116.

Truths About Grieving

Your grief is unique.

Your grief is not linear.

You may travel the same geography over and over,

and over again.

There is no road map or blueprint for grief.

There is no precise time frame for grief.

There is no right way to grieve.

Grieve as you can.

There is no returning to what was,

only an opening to what is and will be.

But there is hope.

Below you will find some things I did to help process, open to and journey through my grief. While not meant to be prescriptive, I hope they may give you some ideas or, better yet, free you to journey in ways that are true to you. (Also see exercises on pages 81–83.)

I started early on writing poetry. I had always found journaling to be beneficial, but poetry was new. The first year after Nathan's death, I wrote over 300 poems. I didn't plan to start, nor did I make it into a regular ritual, but wrote when I felt moved, or when the desire arose in response to a particular event or emotion. A number of those poems are included in this book.

For a number of months, I slept in Nathan's bed. I went to his room sometimes and just lay on the bed he had lain in. It brought me a sense of connection.

I kept one of his photo ID's in my wallet. I still have a couple in the front right-hand corner of my desk. I don't look at them as often these days, but I know they are there.

I took showers. I felt more often than not a release of tears, an inner purging, a cleansing as the hot water flowed over me. As you might imagine, showers took on a whole different role, and it became a discipline at times to take a shower and open to the process of grieving that occurred in that space.

I went by the places he worked—Taco Bell, Blockbuster—and drove by his schools, sometimes stopping to let myself feel whatever arose.

I groaned and sighed, trusting the Holy Spirit to communicate my heart to God when there were no words.

When I did have words, I yelled and screamed at God. I wanted God to know how I was feeling, what I was experiencing and what I thought of this God of power, love and grace. One of the things that really bothered me about God was the simple fact that I knew I was still loved, God was involved in my life, and in the end, love and grace would win. Sometimes that really made me angry, and I let God know that too.

We lit seven-day candles for days on end, a reminder of the light Nathan had been in our lives.

I looked through the cards people sent and the photos of those who had attended his memorial service. It wasn't until a few years later that I was able to re-view the video of his life we had assembled for the service.

We had Nathan cremated, his ashes given to us in a box. We still have the box of ashes in our bedroom closet. In the early weeks I would take it down and hold his ashes, sometimes place the box on his skateboard in the garage and give it a push. Grieve as you can, not as you can't.

One day I decided to go through a box we had picked up from his dorm room. We had left it untouched in the garage, until for some reason I felt the need to search through and fondle his things.

His Stuff

My anguish
　　my torment
　　　　my aching heart
led me out into the garage to explore
Nathan's stuff from college.

I am drawn to a box filled with his clothes.
I begin to slowly sift through them

noticing colors
    textures
        smells.
My pace quickens
Anxiety and hope arise
Heart racing, I frantically dig through
    his jeans
        tee-shirts
carelessly tossing them aside.

Nathan, are you in there?

I reach the bottom of the box.
No Nathan to be found.
I collapse in despair
hot tears stream down my face
    falling
        into
            an empty
                box.

These are a few of the strategies I used to help me fully enter into the grieving process. I found it necessary to employ techniques as a way of intentionally opening to and honestly interacting with whatever surfaced during those early days and months. These little vignettes often led to poems as I processed, or became fodder for my soulful prayers.

My hope is that these examples encourage you to try similar techniques that may come more naturally to you. Beth Slevcove in her book, *Broken Hallelujahs*, lists twenty-five different actions for processing grief, including breaking eggs in the bathtub! See pages 81–83 for some additional exercises.

Grieve as you need to grieve, openly and honestly. Don't hold anything back. Acknowledge God's presence with you just as honestly, remembering that whatever surfaces during these times will either lead you toward God (life/healing) or away from God (death/destruction). Once again the choice is yours—a choice you may feel like you are not fully able to make at this time. Please extend grace and patience to yourself while owning that a desire to desire to make a choice is an important starting point.

CHAPTER SEVEN

GRIEF STAGES...OR NOT

As you journey with grief, you may want the reassurance of a roadmap to follow, since so many have traveled this path before you. You are probably somewhat familiar with the insights of Elisabeth Kübler-Ross, who developed the five stages of grief: denial, anger, bargaining, depression and acceptance. As helpful as this map might feel, there is no longer universal agreement regarding the number or composition of stages. If you are still drawn to such schemas, hold them loosely, keeping in mind a number of caveats:

1. The stages are not linear;

2. not everyone goes through all of them, or if they do, not necessarily in the order established;

3. the so-called stages may be repeated again and again, a move "forward" and then inexplicably a fall "backward." The stages, which may not be stages at all, are descriptive not prescriptive, fluid not concrete, and must be regarded as such.

As I've already mentioned, a precise timeline for grieving is nonexistent. The overall journey is different for everyone; however, I can promise you that the overwhelming, debilitating, all-consuming feelings of despair will dissipate over time. Generally, the hardest period to get through is the first two to three months, but this time of profound emotion may extend to be as long as six months. Somewhere after about two to six months, things begin to shift internally. Little by little, the intensity and duration of your torment begins to decrease. You may not even notice it at first, as the pervasive sadness has become so much a part of your identity. This slow progression is not a return to normal, as the old normal no longer exists—this loss will be with you for the rest of your life. But you will learn to live into, and eventually even embrace, a new normal as time passes. Time doesn't heal all wounds; eternity does.

♪ I Think I Just Saw Nathan

It is not unusual to catch sight of your loved one after the death, burial or funeral has occurred. Someone who walks like, resembles or sounds like the person you are desperately missing will come into view and create a mix of feelings from an imagined reality. This "sighting" doesn't indicate insanity or hallucinations, only that the one who is lost is still in your heart and mind. It's not surprising people once believed in ghosts.

I wrote the following poem over six months after Nathan's death, believing and not believing he was gone.

April Fool

April Fool's Day is over.
Somewhere within I had hoped
Nathan might end his cruel hoax,
this misguided practical joke
faking his own death.
All would be forgiven.
All would be forgotten.
But Nathan was a no-show.

Maybe he really is dead
yet
some part of me still wants to believe
he is alive
Maybe next year
maybe on Mother's Day
maybe on Father's Day
maybe on his birthday
he'll
finally
show
up...

CHAPTER EIGHT

ISOLATION AND COMMUNITY—A DELICATE BALANCE

The Cocoon

I have taken up residence in my grief.
It has become my cocoon
insulating me from life as usual
and bringing a heightened awareness
of sorrow's torturous movements.
Relentlessly, its intensity
generates a transforming energy—
a metamorphosis.

I suffer

Though others surround me
though others weep with me
though others are present to me

I suffer alone

though others have lost loved ones
though my children have lost a brother
though my wife has lost a son

I suffer alone

No one can know my pain
No one can hold my pain

I suffer alone
but I thank God
I am not alone

It is natural for a person in the depths of grief to isolate, to avoid encounters that might lead to more pain. The vulnerability of someone so broken is difficult to explain and harder to navigate, even when relationships are trusted and intimate. In the earliest stages, I wanted to curl up into a ball, to withdraw from all others—a natural tendency for an introvert in protection mode. While self-protection isn't wrong in and of itself, the need for the support of friends and family is real. Such is the dance and the challenge of grief—time alone and time with trusted others.

I created a very small inner circle of individuals who had unfettered access to me, people with whom I had a prior relationship and didn't feel the need to be other than myself. I did not worry about their well-being, but trusted they would process as needed outside of our times together. Their presence did not inhibit me, but in some ways freed me to share or to not share as I saw fit. It was clear that they had only my interest at heart with no expectations or agenda. They were an enormous gift.

My more extroverted wife, Donna, allowed a greater number of people access. Some of them were not safe people to be around during a time of grief, and the things they said were deeply wounding. Donna gave them the benefit of the doubt; she deflected their words as well as she could. For that generosity she paid a great price, suffering significantly in addition to the pain of losing her son. Her stress strengthened my resolve to keep my inner circle small. Fortunately, many of my circle were also people with whom she felt safe and comfortable, which is not always the case. I will address the individuality of spouses grieving separately later.

Although solitude is necessary and beneficial, isolation carries an inherent danger, as unhealthy ways of coping can have long-term negative results. If, like me, you have a tendency to isolate, you will need to continue to make a conscious effort to let people into your space and to share with them what you are feeling. I was fortunate to have a couple of dear friends who were very intentional about being a part of my journey. These special friends were a gift of grace from God, and I am forever grateful to them.

As solitude is necessary, so community is necessary, which raises the question of access. People are either safe or unsafe, and it is helpful if you can predetermine who is in which camp. Not everyone needs equal access; not everyone can be trusted with your vulnerability and pain. Some may be prone to fix, give advice, judge or defend God. I would suggest you err on the side of caution and expand thoughtfully. It's easier to start with a small circle and grow it than to decrease the number midstream, causing pain for all involved.

Having determined who they are, it is as critically important to allow safe people into your life as it is to keep unsafe people out. Sadly, this filter process can be more difficult for Christians, as well-meaning Christians will want to rush in wherever there is pain. The question is, "Who is a safe person?" I have listed below a number of characteristics, but they are only suggestions; you will want to establish your own safety criteria, starting with prior intimate relationships and spreading outward to include trained professionals, such as pastors, counselors and spiritual directors.

Note that family and friends will surprise and disappoint you; our journey produced both. Seek to be open to God's surprises and choose to focus on the people who are present, rather than expending energy on those who, for whatever reason, do not show up—who are unable to show up. At some point down the road, you may need to forgive someone, but it's not a consideration in the early stages of your journey. Your own heart is the one in need of protection and care.

- A safe person is able to be present in the moment with you and to you, able to weep or rejoice as needed.
- A safe person does not feel a need to fix or rescue you.
- A safe person is comfortable with silence, tears, expressed anger, even anger directed toward God.
- A safe person will allow you to freely express and process as you must, without feeling compelled to defend God or correct your theology.
- A safe person is willing to be impacted and changed by your loss.
- A safe person will practice confidentiality.
- A safe person is able to be in the mess and the uncertainty of the grieving process.
- A safe person is able to trust God and the process, knowing God is at work in the circumstances.
- A safe person can entrust you to God.
- A safe person can hold hope, faith and joy for you as needed.[6]

The type of person described above is of immeasurable help, both initially and also through the years. These individuals give you the gift of their presence and allow you to be you, to feel and express as you need to, whether with tears, anger, frustration, or laughter. The only agenda they bring is to be a companion for the uncharted journey with grief.

---

6. Slevcove, page 179.

Note: If you discover that someone already in the mix is not safe, you need to establish and maintain new boundaries. If you aren't able to make the change yourself, ask for help from someone who can.

Chapter Nine

Grief Brain

The first several months after Nathan's death were marked by a disconcerting inability in myself to concentrate, remember, or think logically. I learned this mental condition is commonly referred to as "grief brain," a very real, thankfully temporary, symptom of grief that leaves one wandering in a fog, unable to process or complete the simplest tasks. It is wise to avoid significant decisions, as even the most mundane may be problematic. During our grief brain period, we kept two boxes for mail: one held mail we wished to keep and look through later and another for mail to be discarded after one more sorting. We could not trust ourselves to even make a decision regarding our mail, since simply opening the envelopes could feel overwhelming at times. At other times, it was a wonderful distraction.

A rule of thumb after suffering loss is to not make any major decisions (moving, job change, what to keep or discard) during the first year after the death of a loved one. While not a hard-and-fast rule, it does reflect the reality that one's ability to think has, to some degree, been compromised by loss and emotional stress. This period of healing requires patience and grace with one's self, as well as a disciplined withdrawal from decisions that might have long-term implications. The choice to rush the process is unhealthy and unwise and may be motivated by a desire to escape the pervasive pain. Resist the pressure to get on with life—please, no major decisions.

CHAPTER TEN

SIX FOUNDATIONAL PASSAGES

Words

He is in heaven
He is happy
He is with Jesus
All things work together for good...

Like spit on a hot grill
are traditional words of comfort
They dance on the surface
soon to evaporate into nothingness
but
Like water poured out onto a dry sponge
two words penetrate
> *my heart*
> *my soul*
> *my spirit*

"Jesus wept"

Jesus grieves with me
Jesus embraces me and my sorrow

Jesus doesn't rush to the truth of the resurrection

Jesus sits with me
feels with me
hurts with me
weeps with me

Jesus weeps

an invitation to tarry in my grief
an invitation to embrace my
sorrow
anguish
questions
anger
confusion

Jesus weeps
he cares
he is with me
he knows my pain
he knows me

Jesus weeps and so do I
Hallelujah

The six scripture passages below freed me to journey openly with grief, unapologetically honest with God, myself and selected others. Scripture allowed me to trust God and trust the process during those times I was overwhelmed by despair, when God seemed distant and I felt so very, very alone. These passages reminded me that I was not alone, that somewhere in the freefall of despair, God had placed a safety net, even though it was invisible to me at the time.

The passage that meant the most to me, that brought me the greatest freedom and solace, is also the shortest verse in the Bible: "Jesus wept" (John 11:35). The fact that Jesus shed tears over the death of his friend, knowing that in a matter of moments he would raise him from the dead, freed me to shed tears for my son. Even while I knew this tragic loss was not the end, while I believed deep down in God's promise of hope and resurrection, I was comforted by Jesus' tears. Jesus knew my pain, not in the abstract, but in the concrete reality of his relationship with his own friend. I did not weep alone; Jesus was with me, understanding the depth of my suffering, not seeking to rush me through it, but choosing to be with me in it.

The following two passages, which describe Jesus' interactions with God during emotionally demanding times in his own life, allowed me to be honest with God about my feelings and my current experience of God. I was able to speak to God with unedited, raw honesty, not fearing God's response, but knowing God would hear me and be with me in the messiness of my unimaginable anguish.

And He went a little beyond them, and fell on His face and prayed, saying, "My Father, if it is possible, let this cup pass from Me; yet not as I
will, but as You will" (Matthew 26:39, NASB).

About the ninth hour Jesus cried out with a loud voice, saying, "Eli,
Eli, lama sabachthani?" that is, "My God, My God, why have You
forsaken Me?" (Matthew 27:46, NASB).

In these passages Jesus does not hold back, but freely expresses his experience.
God, where did you go? These pure expressions of emotion made a huge impact
on me, freeing me to go to God just as I was in the moment, sharing a torrent of
feelings about my circumstances, and even my opinion of and rage toward God.
(Note: The above passages are elaborated on further in Section Two—see pages
124–125).

Romans 8:26-27 brought me great comfort. I knew during the periods I could not
pray that the Holy Spirit was praying on my behalf, whispering my unarticulated
prayers deep into the heart of the Triune God.

In the same way the Spirit also helps our weakness; for we do not know
how to pray as we should, but the Spirit Himself intercedes for us with
groanings too deep for words; and He who searches the hearts knows
what the mind of the Spirit is, because He intercedes for the saints according to the will of God (NASB).

The final two passages formed the foundation upon which my entire journey
with grief was built. These passages stabilized me when someone cast doubts
or reacted negatively to my ranting. These passages assured me that God could
handle my emotions.

For I am convinced that neither death, nor life, nor angels, nor principalities, nor things present, nor things to come, nor powers, nor height, nor
depth, nor any other created thing, will be able to separate us from the
love of God, which is in Christ Jesus our Lord (Romans 8:38-39, NASB).

Therefore there is now no condemnation for those who are in Christ
Jesus (Romans 8:1, NASB).

These passages remind us that we cannot be separated from God's love—period!
Additionally, because of who we are in Christ, we cannot, will not, receive any
condemnation from God. No matter what I say to God, I will be loved, not con-
demned. This is the freedom we have to be open and honest with God.

Finally, the examples of Job and the Psalmists were also very helpful, for each expressed their heartfelt feelings: Job questioning and accusing God, and the Psalmist doing the same in some most unflattering ways. See two examples below:

> How long, O Lord? Will You forget me forever? How long will You hide Your face from me? (Psalm 13:1, NASB).

> I am bowed down and brought very low; all day long I go about mourning. My back is filled with searing pain; there is no health in my body. I am feeble and utterly crushed; I groan in anguish of heart (Psalm 38:6-8, NIV).

Many other Psalms articulate the cries of the suffering—of those who feel far from God or abandoned by God. They actually give permission, even encourage us to express anger toward and accusations of God in the reality of human despair. Praise God for the gift of scripture.

Jerry Sittser writes:

> The God I know has experienced pain and therefore understands my pain. In Jesus I have felt God's tears, trembled before his death on the cross, and witnessed the redemptive power of his suffering.... I have grieved long and hard and intensely. But I have found comfort in knowing that the sovereign God...is the same God who has experienced the pain I live with everyday.[7]

And Nicholas Wolterstorff reminds us that, "God is not only the God of the sufferers but the God who suffers,"[8] and also that, "God is suffering love."[9]

My hope is that the above passages will remind you that God is with you no matter what, and that this knowledge will free you to express yourself to God with unedited honesty, certain of God's faithful presence with you and sustaining love for you.

---

7. Sittser, page 158.
8. Wolterstorff, page 81.
9. Wolterstorff, page 90.

🎵 I Believe, Help Me in My Unbelief

The statements below concerning you and God are true. Like gravity, they just are, whether you believe them or not, whether you feel them or not—may they help stabilize you in the storms of sorrow.

- God is with you in your pain and sorrow.
- God weeps with you.
- You cannot be separated from God.
- You cannot be separated from God's love.
- God is faithful, even if you are faithless.
- The Holy Spirit prays for you when you are unable to pray.
- God will bring good out of your situation.
- God will use your situation to transform you.
- God desires honesty.
- God's grace is present.
- There is love, grace and hope.

CHAPTER ELEVEN

GRIEF AND HOPE

The foundational truths found in the following passages can, if you let them, encourage and empower you to more fully enter into your current experience in truth, enabled to put your trust in God and in the healing process. They, like the passages in the previous chapter, encourage honesty and free you to approach God openly, to turn toward God, life and healing. I share these all-important words of scripture with the hope that you will not escape in them, but will use them as fuel to continue to move forward on your journey.

This first familiar passage is one I sometimes hated early in my journey with grief, especially when others threw it at me with a hurtful glibness, seeking to apply it as a spiritual bandage to cover my pain. This passage is often used a little too quickly, and in its familiarity, it may prompt you or others to circumvent what God desires to accomplish through difficulty. As I said, in my grief, I had a love/hate relationship with this verse—when people use verses like this cheaply, they cause pain. Rest in the fact that God uses his words differently. At such times of deep and pervasive suffering, I believe only God can speak authoritatively into our hearts and our hurt.

> And we know that in all things God works for the good of those who love him, who have been called according to his purpose (Romans 8:28).

The truth of this passage angered me, since I wasn't ready to acknowledge this "good news" reality. In order to be honest about my feelings and honest with God, I had to admit I was not at all ready to allow my pain to dissipate prematurely. I somehow wanted to remain in the valley of loneliness and suffering, not willing to consider God's promise of a positive outcome. But I believed down deep in that promise and would eventually be ready to claim it.

The passages below are also helpful reminders that death is not the end of the story; God is bigger and greater than anything you are currently experiencing, even the death of a loved one. Hope, grace and love are always present, whether we feel it, want to acknowledge it or even currently believe it. Such is the beauty of truth: like gravity, it is just there, keeping our feet planted, even as our world is spinning out of control.

But we do not want you to be uninformed, brethren, about those who are asleep, *that you will not grieve as do the rest who have no hope* (1 Thessalonians 4:13, NASB (emphasis mine).

I consider that our present sufferings are not worth comparing with the glory that will be revealed in us (Romans 8:18).

"'He will wipe every tear from their eyes. There will be no more death' or mourning or crying or pain, for the old order of things has passed away" (Revelation 21:4).

For Now

Resurrection
life-everlasting
heaven
These words bring
no consolation
no comfort
no peace
no hope
they are merely words.

I do not doubt their truth
but for now they hold no power over
my heart
my sorrow
my sadness
my grief
my despair

One day I will treasure them
One day I will bank my hope on them
One day they will be ambassadors of
consolation
comfort
peace

That day is not now
That day may be far away
For now, they are mere words.
They hold no power.

CHAPTER TWELVE

HONEST TO GOD

I began writing poetry within the first few days after Nathan's death. Compelled to be unconditionally and agonizingly honest, I lashed out with anger and frustration. Although I couldn't feel God's presence, I was angry that I was unable to distance myself from the knowledge of God's unconditional love. I felt free to express my anger, even hatred, knowing deep inside that God was with me in love and compassion, not angry with me for my words or accusations. I knew the safety net of God's presence was down there somewhere, as I tumbled in my freefall of grief.

Hate

God, I hate you
I hate you
I hate you

thank you
for
inviting, welcoming
my
raw, naked, unabashed
honesty

God, I love you

Where

God, where were you
why didn't you do something
what were you thinking

my son is dead
and I know

you were watching
you were there and
did nothing to save him

what were you thinking
what were you feeling

my son is dead and I know
you were there with him

God, You Stink

My son is dead
I hate this
this loss
this sadness
this ache
I hate that
in the midst of my anguish
I know and experience
       your love
       your grace
       your mercy
Anger bubbles within
yet I know and experience
       your goodness
       your care
       your presence
My son is dead
I hate this
use it for your glory and praise
I am overwhelmed by
       my grief
       my sorrow
       my loss
Use it to make me more like Jesus
God, you stink
but I love that

I can be
  angry
  upset
  totally honest with you
My son is dead
I hate this
But I love you, God

ANGER

Anger is something you may powerfully experience as you process the loss of a loved one. Your anger may be directed toward some or all of the following: the deceased, your spouse, the person/entity you view as responsible (doctor, killer, drunk driver, police, hospital, government, etc.), God and even yourself.

Anger is natural and should not be suppressed. Process your anger with someone who will listen, and who will refrain from comment or judgment, ideally a trained therapist, pastor, spiritual director, support group, or trusted friend. Journaling can be helpful, and so can other methods of creatively expressing your feelings directly to God.

God desires your honesty. Don't stuff it by ignoring your feelings, distracting yourself, or making unhealthy coping and numbing choices (e.g., Traps to Avoid, page 29), but rather choose to use whatever you are feeling, experiencing your emotions as a prompt to turn toward God, toward healing and toward life.

CHAPTER THIRTEEN

A CRITICAL QUESTION

In the years since my son's death, I have repeatedly asked myself, "Is what I am currently feeling or experiencing taking me toward God (healing and life) or away from God (despair and death)?" This critical self-assessment is helpful in any season, but would have been invaluable during the first year following Nathan's death. My hope is you will make time to reflect on this question at least daily, as it provides a steady base against the whiplash of grief—the onslaught of sorrow, moments of relief, debilitating rage followed by gratitude for the memories and everything in between.

At first this self-reflection may not come easily, but I encourage you to continue as you are able; once a week is better than not at all. Trust in the God of loaves and fish, bringing what you have, doing what you can, expecting God to receive and multiply what you offer (cf. Matthew 14:17-20). Start by opening to God in honesty, acknowledging God's love for you and presence with you. God is sustaining you and weeping with you, whether you feel it or not.

I wasn't surprised that some of my past emotions resurfaced during the process of writing this book, but the passage of time and emotional healing have given me new tools for this journey. I relied on the question above for stability and direction, finding Matthew 14:28-31a encouraging:

"Lord, if it's you," Peter replied, "tell me to come to you on the water."

"Come," he said.

Then Peter got down out of the boat, walked on the water and came toward Jesus. But when he saw the wind, he was afraid and, beginning to sink, cried out, "Lord, save me!"

Immediately Jesus reached out his hand and caught him.

Peter asked to walk on the water, and Jesus invited him to do so. Peter got out of the boat and walked on water. He did it! "Then Peter got down out of the boat, walked on the water and came toward Jesus. But when he saw the wind, he was afraid and, beginning to sink, cried out, 'Lord, save me!'" (v. 29b-30). Peter lost his focus and began to pay attention to the wind and waves to such a degree that he took his eyes off Jesus and began to sink. Now the wind and the waves were there from the beginning, but at first they were not Peter's sole focus. I'm not saying he didn't feel them, did not know they were all around him, but he was not focused on them. For a time, his primary focus was on Jesus, before he became overwhelmed by the wind and the waves.

The question, "Is this taking me toward God or away from God?" helps you to maintain your Jesus-focus in the midst of the wind and waves. It does not mean you don't feel the force of the them, but rather you let what you're feeling become a reminder to go toward Jesus in the midst of the turbulence. Trust the God of loaves and fish to meet you where you are with the promise, "I can work with that."

Finally, draw solace from the end of the passage, "But when he saw the wind, he was afraid and, beginning to sink, cried out, 'Lord, save me!' Immediately Jesus reached out his hand and caught him" (Matthew 14:30-31a). Peter's experience of sinking, overwhelmed by the wind and the waves, led him to cry out to Jesus for saving. Jesus heard and responded by reaching out his hand.

Although I did not have this critical question in mind in my early stages of grief, I allowed my poetry to turn me toward God. My poems shared my heart freely and honestly with God, keeping my focus on the God of life and healing. See exercises on pages 81–83 for additional ways to process. It is important to find ways that are true to who you are.

Why My Son?

God, why my son?
Why not another?
Why not a child molester
*   a drug addict*
*   a murderer*
*   a devil worshipper?*

Why my son?
*   he was dedicated to you as a baby*

baptized as a child
he had a hopeful future
Why my son?
    is it something I did
    something I didn't do?
    Is it my punishment—
    the result of my past sin
    or my current imperfections?

God, do you hear me? Are you there?

Why my son?
    you delivered Abraham's son
    you brought Lazarus back from the grave
    you raised Jairus' daughter

My son is dead—still dead
Why my son?
    was it too much trouble
    were you too busy
    did you have a wager going with Satan?

Is this some kind of test—
a way of seeing if I truly love you?

Why my son?

Chapter Fourteen

Dangerous Questions

"What if? If only…I should have…" These self-incriminating questions will undoubtedly erupt at some point, often forcefully, leading to regret and anguish. I don't think it is possible to avoid some element of responsibility, regardless of the circumstances or rationality. I was attacked by self-doubt at all times of the day and night, but especially when I was really tired and worn down, when I was unable to fight back. "If only…I should have…" stole the little strength I had gained.

"I should have said good-bye to Nathan that final day. I should have told him more often that I loved him, was proud of him. If only I did not let him go away to college. If only I would have bought him a cell phone, called him more often, spent more time with him, given him a car. What if…"

Since avoiding the repetitive, painful attack of dangerous questioning is unlikely, it's important to be aware of your reactions, of what is being stirred up inside. Is what I'm feeling taking me to God or away from God? As discussed earlier, this self-reflection is helpful anytime, but it is essential when starting down this unhealthy road. Remember, in the midst of this dangerous questioning, just asking the good question turns your attention to God; if you realize that you are beginning to sink in the waves of "what if, if only, I should have," cry out to Jesus for help. Know the Holy Spirit is praying for you, God is with you, and love and grace are God's gift to you.

Regrets

If only's
should've's
echo through the valley
of my soul
causing an avalanche of regrets

CHAPTER FIFTEEN

AVOIDING OR COPING

Most of us are not fans of pain, but often pain is inescapable, as in the pain of great loss. When I look at photographs from that first year, I can clearly see pain in my wife's eyes, the grief etched in the lines of her face, and I know my face reflected the same message. It is natural to desire to escape pain, to make choices that—while not totally eliminating pain—will numb it, will enable a temporary outlet. A go-to strategy for me was always movies or television, but in my newly acquired awareness after Nathan died, even that wasn't foolproof. I remember being shocked by the number of characters on screen who were routinely run down by a car or truck. While watching a recommended comedy, I was horrified to see a person be obliterated by a bus, as he was innocently standing in the street. I can still see that image now as I type.

While grief is not to be avoided, it is helpful to escape from the pain and mourning periodically. But escape can be a two-edged sword, especially since grief is accompanied by a tendency to withdraw and isolate. Also, as with any coping behavior, escape modes fall into healthy and unhealthy; even a behavior that begins as healthy can, through overuse, become unhealthy. Avoidance may turn into running away from—a suppression of the natural manifestation of grief. But grief, when entered into, brings healing and the ability to embrace life's new reality.

Our culture offers many acceptable escape methods to avoid the pain and questions brought to the surface by grief. The most common are consuming food, taking drugs, immersing in work, movies and TV, mindless reading/shopping/spending, alcohol and even exercise. Take the desire, conscious or unconscious, to get through this discomfort and return to normal (a place that no longer exists), and add it to the fact that your family and friends can become enablers, encouraging behavior that, while not illegal or overtly unhealthy, is derailing your journey, and you might find yourself immobilized in the grip of coping mechanisms that keep you from engaging your grief and moving forward.

Food became my place of soothing and relief. Food had been a comfort to me before, but this time it was different. Food was an acceptable and accessible coping mechanism, easily supported by everyone in our community and encouraged by people who cared deeply for me. I gained weight—a lot of weight. My unhealthy dependence on food stayed with me until recently and, while writing this book, I could once again hear the siren call of food beckoning me.

When it comes to coping or distracting behavior, it is helpful to have a person who knows you well and who can share their observations with you honestly, graciously speaking to you in love and truth. It's easy to fool yourself, to excuse, justify or minimize your behavior, and most people will be afraid to offend or upset, "especially now." A faithful friend, spiritual director, or pastor can be extremely helpful, as I do not think we can be trusted to monitor our coping techniques on our own.

Below are some behaviors that can circumvent the healing process. Be aware of the temptations and be intentional about avoiding them as means of escaping grief. Some can be extremely destructive; some are socially acceptable. Consider why a certain behavior is inviting, and practice moderation in the acceptable coping mechanisms; abstain from the destructive ones.

- Busyness, no space for genuine grieving
- Food (consuming or denying)
- An invincible front, not allowing others to join in your suffering
- The use of scripture to suppress feelings
- Use of God and faith as spiritual numbing
- Drugs
- Blaming and shaming yourself
- Turning to others to take away your pain
- Blaming others
- Avoiding/denying your suffering
- Alcohol
- Mindless reading
- Isolating from God and others
- Movies, television, internet, gaming
- Porn, gambling and other non-substance addictions
- Nursing your anger

All the behaviors above can distance you from God and prevent you from experiencing God's presence in your pain, from claiming the strength that emerges out of your weakness. God told Paul, "My grace is sufficient for you, for my power is made perfect in weakness" (2 Corinthians 12:9b). When you're in deep, emotional pain, it can be tempting to try to numb your feelings with drugs, alcohol, food, or even work. Be careful—these temporary escapes won't lead to faster healing, but may lead to addiction, depression, anxiety, or even an emotional breakdown.

Instead, use the suggestions below to help you come to terms with your loss and begin to heal:

- Give yourself time. Accept your feelings and know that grieving is a process.
- Talk to others. Spend time with friends and family. Don't isolate.
- Take care of yourself—exercise, eat well and get enough sleep.
- Do some of the things you have previously enjoyed.
- Use whatever you are feeling or experiencing to take you to God.
- Visit a support group.

CHAPTER SIXTEEN

BIRTHDAY AND ANNIVERSARY OF DEATH

FIRST BIRTHDAY

The questions loomed: How would we celebrate this first birthday without him? Would we do something? Would we do nothing? How would we feel? The thought of the date approaching consumed us—the thought of revisiting his birth and, of course, his death. It seemed still that his death trumped his life. The loss, not as painful eight months in, still defined my relationship with Nathan, still dictated my thoughts and feelings toward him.

It is at such an occasion that "should" and "shouldn't" can gain power, and you may feel you are being forced into something you don't have the desire or the emotional energy to do. Please, above all, remember to grieve as you need to grieve. The truth is you don't know what you will feel on that day, so it is a good idea to make some contingency plans that may or may not be executed. Give yourself freedom to change everything the day of, and communicate your intention to be flexible to all involved.

In our first year, Nathan's birthday sort of snuck up on me. We chose not to have a traditional birthday party with cake, but we did decide to acknowledge him with the food he enjoyed on special occasions. That first birthday, and every year since, we celebrated him with Asian cuisine (from a very young age, he requested Asian food for his birthday) and chocolate chip cookies. (He had tried many times, unsuccessfully, to make chocolate chip cookies, but the memories, not the cookies, are what we treasure.) Our intentional food choice acknowledged and celebrated the gift he was to us for eighteen years. We also touched base with all of our kids, which is something we continue to do. Each birthday we share what we are planning and a reflection about Nathan.

Ask yourself, do you want to actively remember/celebrate the birthday this year? If no, what might you do that day? Also, you may want to share your decision with others, freeing them to do something on their own and creating space for you. If yes, how do you intend to remember and celebrate the birth of your loved one? Would you like company? If yes, who?

Remember, it's yours to decide; grieve as you can, not as you cannot. If you don't want to be alone, but also do not want a celebration of any kind, let it be known among your trusted companions. There is no way to anticipate your feelings ahead of time—what your feelings will be on the day of, or the day after—and the experience may be different from year to year.

ONE-YEAR ANNIVERSARY OF THE DEATH

There is no right way or wrong way to go about this day. As the first anniversary approached, I had no desire to revisit the excruciating pain of a year earlier, the day that had left our family devastated. I wanted to ignore it altogether, but a friend at our church suggested I acknowledge Nathan's life on that day, rather than his death, replacing that day of loss with a day of commemoration. So we did. Painfully, we forced ourselves to begin to focus on the life lived, rather than the life lost. Filled with overwhelming sadness and sorrow, shedding many tears, I believe we felt a subtle shift begin to take place. I assembled a little memory box of sorts. I'm not even sure what it was I collected for it, but I do remember that the experience of thinking through the contents, in order to communicate something about Nathan, was in itself helpful. Also, since Nathan was killed in the early morning hours of Halloween, we began giving away entire bags of candy to the children who came to our door. He had loved to accumulate candy, so we commemorate him in that decadent way to this day.

Again, the same questions apply: Do you want to actively remember the day of the death of your loved one? If no, what might you do that day? Also, you may want to share your decision with others, freeing them to do something on their own and creating space for you. If yes, how will you remember and celebrate not the death, but the life of your loved one? Would you like company? If yes, who?

The anniversary is yours to acknowledge or ignore, but I encourage you to be open to expression, even though it will be painful. Healing often is. The act of commemoration was an enormous step forward for me. The emotions of grief are like waves in the ocean: they come and go, and you don't always know when or why. Acknowledge your feelings and let them take you to God.

CHAPTER SEVENTEEN

HOLIDAYS

If you belong to a family, you probably have some holiday traditions. Unlike the birthday and death anniversary we spoke of previously, family holiday traditions carry with them expectations. Navigating this first round will take some intentional communication and may cause additional issues and pain to arise, especially if children are involved.

My son died on October 31 and the memorial service was one week later, on November 8, my wife's birthday. Nineteen days after that, Thanksgiving occurred, and twenty-eight days later came Christmas. We went through the first round of holidays deeply mired in grief. Typically, the first few months are about survival, coping, getting out of bed, remembering to eat, shower and living through the hellishness of loss. For us, the holidays were an endless nightmare of pain and suffering, each a reminder of how our life had changed for the worse, of what we no longer were.

The pallor of sadness colored everything and everyone. All I remember of that first Christmas is absence—no tree, no decorations, no Nathan. I think we did attend an annual Christmas party that our lifelong friends had been throwing every year for decades, but I could not swear to it. I do remember that our Thanksgiving table had a place set for Nathan, a moment of silence and not much else.

Remembering that grief is unique, and your experience may be very different from mine, the message I want to make clear is, if you are able, propose a game plan for navigating the holidays. It may be helpful to have two plans: plan A is what you hope will happen, and plan B is what you will do if you aren't able to pull off plan A. Communicate both plans to everyone involved, even the possibility that, at some point, you may need to leave the gathering and take a personal time-out. Since holidays often involve extended family members and friends, advance communication is really helpful. If you don't feel up to doing it yourself, ask someone else to speak on your behalf. Choosing to talk things through ahead of time helps others to be thoughtful in their preparations, freeing you to be in the moment, secure in the knowledge that you have two plans ready.

The first year and first holiday may be incredibly difficult, or not. Each holiday is different, and each situation is personal, depending on the amount of time that has passed, the age of the individual who died, the role that person played at the gathering. I have friends who looked forward to the first Christmas without an elderly parent, even though the death itself impacted them deeply. While alive, the parent had made the holiday almost unbearable, and that first Christmas freed them to host and creatively celebrate the one who passed. It was a lovely and touching evening.

As always, family dynamics influence decisions around and outcomes of holiday planning. Young children may not fully grasp the gravity of the event, and emotions often cause conflict to arise between spouses and between siblings, when all are not able to agree on how best to proceed. Grieving is difficult, and families are often the same. The navigation of holidays can be messy, but planning ahead, knowing your limits and communicating your plans will eliminate some of the stress.

If you have lost a parent or a child or a spouse (a co-parent), Mother's Day and Father's Day can be extremely painful, not only the first year, but for many years to come. Once again, it is wise to prepare yourself ahead of time, realistically thinking through the events of the day in light of the makeup of your family and your emotional disposition. Also, take time to consider your presence with the one who may be more deeply impacted by the particular holiday—your spouse, the surviving mother or father, your children. Be assured God is present in your togetherness.

Below are some questions to use as prompts when contemplating your holidays:

What is your hope/goal for the holiday this year? Is it to focus on the individual, the occasion or both? What is your mental and emotional capacity? Do you prefer to remember your loved one privately or publicly, with immediate family or involving other family members or friends? Will you exchange gifts? Would you consider donations made in memory of your loved one?

Thanksgiving

Thanksgiving
a family gathered
minus one

an empty place
a missing plate
a time of silence

Unwrapped Box

A box lay under the Christmas tree
A box containing what once brought
joy
laughter
and fun into our lives

but no more.

The box reminds us of
past joys
present sorrow
future sadness.

The box contains a gift that was given
by God 18 years ago.

The box contains the ashes of my son.

Easter

Easter has come and gone
but the chasm between my head and heart
remains as daunting as ever.

My incantations:
"He is risen! He is risen indeed!"
worked no magic.
merely words of intellectual assent
causing nothing within.

The chasm remains.

✤ Just Say No

The holiday season is always full of additional pressure, but for one in the throes of grief, the real or felt obligations and expectations can be crushing. Practice self-care by ridding yourself of all unwanted obligations: hosting, attending parties (or a particular party), buying presents, sending cards, traveling, participating in church services. Instead, choose only the activities that may bring you some level of enjoyment or that feel safe, bearable.

Following the loss of a loved one, you have choices to make; make them without guilt. Be intentional about owning your limitations.

CHAPTER EIGHTEEN

VENTURING OUT

At some point I decided to escape the sadness and safety of our home and venture out to the store for the first time. Being in public was difficult for me, an emotionally unstable introvert. At home I could let myself go, but outside I felt fragile and exposed. I had no idea who I would see or who would see me, what another person might say to me or how I would respond. I had already experienced some negative encounters, so I knew both friend and foe could be a threat to my psyche. I also knew the power of the rogue waves of grief and was not eager to be washed out to sea emotionally while getting some groceries.

Our home, my protective cocoon, was beginning to feel like a prison, and I needed to see something other than my wife's sad eyes. As I walked into the store, I felt the need to punch someone; I hoped someone would say something, anything, so I could answer with a punch in the face. Taking in the array of products, my emotions were triggered by a number of the foods, such as eggnog and chocolate chip cookie mix. Grief is the ultimate shape-shifter, able to take the form of anything. When I checked out, I was unsure how to answer the question, "Did you find everything you were looking for?" I wanted my son back, my family not hurting, relief from the pain and sorrow, and that was nowhere to be found.

I was flummoxed by the decision between paper or plastic...but I survived. I returned to my cocoon and to my cry, and allowed all I was feeling to surface, reflecting on the sweet memories attached to eggnog and chocolate chip cookies.

Once again, grief is a unique experience, so mine may not be anything like yours. I share this particular memory, because any public space can be a minefield, especially if you are carrying a lot of anger or if you are depleted. If you feel the need or desire to go out, think through the questions that will likely come up and plan your answers. For instance, when meeting someone for the first time, a natural question is, "How many children do you have?" often followed by, "Where do they live? What do they do?" Would I answer "three" or "four"? If four, how would I answer the follow-up question? Over time, I devised a plan. I decided to say four, then answer the follow-up question without naming Nathan. This plan has worked for me, and since I have said, "I have four children," no one has ever asked, "What about the other one?" Or, "That was just three."

I hope you are recognizing a theme emerging in the last few chapters: think ahead and prepare—the best you can with grief brain—for all that lies ahead, whether it be running errands or surviving birthdays and holidays. As you are able, give thought and try to prepare yourself for the next undertaking, knowing that it can go sideways pretty quickly.

Outside

Forays into the world of people
  are fraught with danger
            no control over comments
                    questions

As I remain in seclusion
    The bars grow thicker
            stronger
                    with each passing day.

Triggers

Images, sounds, smells
  reminding me of times long past
  of feelings simmering
  just beneath the surface

to never-again's
  and never-shall-be's

Drawing out pain
  sorrow, anguish

ending in tears
  new realizations of loss, sadness

Inviting me to remember,
  embrace, grieve

to sit with the memory
the thought
the feeling
exploring, mining, savoring

Open to finding God
finding myself
finding healing

CHAPTER NINETEEN

CHANGING RELATIONSHIP WITH THE DECEASED

I'm not sure how it happens and haven't seen much written, but I do know from personal experience, and the experience of others, that one's relationship with the deceased person usually changes after death. It is common to remember all the good, the endearing, the noble and what was worthy of praise in an unconscious process of canonization. The memories, while not false, largely ignore the negative characteristics of the person and of the relationship; the life of the deceased is not being fully fleshed out. There is nothing wrong with this celebration of good; in fact, it is a time-honored practice, out of respect, to not speak ill of the dead.

The important thing here is to be aware of the healing process taking place when you hear yourself owning more of the fullness of who this human being really was. When conversations with others reveal less of the ascribed saint-like qualities, you will know the landscape within your heart is changing, indicating a measure of healing. This change is not something you can will or work toward, but a gradual restoration for you to notice, as you are sharing with trusted family and friends.

Pay attention to your descriptions of your loved one, to the incidents you are willing to feel, face and share. I remember one day talking about Nathan to a dear friend, one who had been with me from the beginning, admitting what a pain Nathan could be and giving exasperating examples about conflicts with teachers and long, pointless arguments with my wife just to be contrary. My dear friend astutely pointed out that my sharing about Nathan had changed. I don't know if I would have noticed or not, but it was extremely helpful to have it called to my attention. This conversation also affirms the value of having family and friends on the journey with you.

Afterward, I realized I was thinking of Nathan at all stages of his life, not only when he was little (which is how I often saw him in my dreams). I began to remember him over all the eighteen years he was with us, owning the good, the bad and the annoying. I could look at pictures of him and feel a mix of emotions—sorrow and joy, gratitude and even hope, and I was encouraged that my heart was beginning to heal. By paying attention to my shifting feelings, I was reminded that God was at work and reminded to trust God with my healing process.

CHAPTER TWENTY

WORDS AND FEELINGS

Sometimes it's difficult to name what you are feeling, so I have provided a list of feeling words and phrases that may help. Read through the list, choosing one or more that resonates with your experience. Then try to define it—what does it specifically mean to you? Where do you feel it in your body? How heavy is it? Is it possible to hand it to God or to ask God for help to carry it? Use this list as you journal, and write psalms and laments or poetry (see pages 82–83).

Words for the Grief Journey

numbness, emptiness, loneliness, disbelief, unbelief, isolation, together, alone, relief, fear, anxiety, guilt, shame, Jesus, confusion, tears, doubt, disappointment, anger, ache, heartache, sadness, despair, moaning, grief brain (loss of ability to concentrate, short-term memory loss), vulnerable, ignored, joy, sorrow, what if, if only, God, weakness, laughter, sting, bemoan, surrender, overwhelmed, goodbye, broken, wounded, hurting, searching, groaning, avalanche, listen, silent, endure, escape, grateful, trembling, anguish, broken dreams, Holy Spirit, community, sleeplessness, abandonment, forsaken, frustration, fatigue, needed, dread, peace, journey, waves of grief, mourning, lost, death, strength, limitations, scream, sigh, void, uncertain, regret, hope, hopeless, disappointment, rogue waves, shape-shifter....

It was through writing that I began to be able to articulate what I was feeling, to pray, to open up to the journey, to become more present to my wife and children. Writing helped me first discover what I was feeling and then to process those feelings. I invite you to try it, even if you have not been much of a writer prior to this time. Don't worry about spelling or sentence structure; just start honestly expressing your feelings, and see what happens. You may want to try using different colors of ink or drawing pictures, writing one word that fills an entire page or simply listing thoughts as bullet points. There is no wrong way to grieve or pray on paper. This technique helped me to be in touch with my feelings and pray those feelings openly to God, then to take my processing further in poetry. My cries took form, and the poems of my journey emerged.

CHAPTER TWENTY-ONE

A FAMILY AFFAIR

The grieving process takes a huge toll on a marriage and family. As each person's journey with grief is unique, often isolating and not linear, a family's patterns of grieving rarely line up. One family member might be in the grip of sorrow while the other is experiencing a respite, maybe even having a fleeting moment of happiness. Such was the case in our home. We were walking billboards, each graphically displaying the loss and pain we were experiencing. A momentary respite from the grief was quickly crushed by the personification of sorrow witnessed in the other. We each employed different strategies to deal with the pervasiveness of what we were feeling. While I was focused on withdrawing and protecting myself (even at times from my wife), my wife was more open to inviting people in, receiving whatever they offered. All of these newly introduced differences between us caused tension; at times we did not want to be with each other.

And then there was Ricky, our youngest child, a junior in high school, who still lived in the house with us. The other two were older and living on their own. Ricky had lost his older brother, and, virtually, his parents as well. His home was permeated by sadness, his parents struggling separately and together, while he was suffering his own grief. As parents, we were desperately trying to get the oxygen masks on ourselves, essentially unable to help anyone else. This very real incapacity is another reminder of the necessity of involving others to do what we may be temporarily unable to do for ourselves.

As you can imagine, our son did not want to stay in the bleak confines of our home, but the thought of him leaving frightened us well beyond a normal parental concern. We feared for his safety, even that he might be killed; this threat was no longer theoretical. Every minute he was late, we expected the worst.

The separation and isolation brought on by the death of a child or parent is real and needs to be acknowledged and dealt with. At some point, family counseling may be needed; simply naming this possibility can help normalize the experience and reduce tensions.

Let me offer some suggestions that may help relieve tensions in the home:

- Do not judge. Remember, each person grieves differently; resist the temptation to judge the other person's process.

- Look for ways to help one another. As you are able, ask God to help you be with the other person. I was able to help my wife by doing the dishes, and discovered dishwashing was soothing for me as well. Serve without expectation, trusting in the power of your acts of love. Also, receive from your spouse as you are able.

- Choose to be together (take walks, sit, share meals); it's too easy to live under the same roof alone. Ask how the other is doing, even when you don't feel like engaging.

- Be vocal about your love for one another. This is something I found myself starting right away—verbally declaring (also in writing, in texts, emails and notes) that I loved my family members.

- Process together. Seek to be a support for your spouse and/or your child, a safe place. Share your feelings; communicate your struggles; talk about a helpful process to move forward as a couple or family. Processing together helped us immensely.

- Practice physical demonstrations of love. As a married couple, it is especially important to maintain physical intimacy during this time—holding hands, hugging and meeting the other's sexual needs as you are able. It can be tricky, as one or both of you may feel receiving comfort is a betrayal of sorts. If so, talk about your feelings and process them together.

- Pray—make it a priority to pray individually for your spouse and children in their grief. As you open yourself to God, God will give you insights as to how to creatively love and serve your loved ones.

- Pray together as a couple and as a family.

- Continue to care for yourself. Beware of isolating; take time to reflect and give attention and love to those who are still with you.

- Pay attention to the ongoing dynamics of your marriage and family relations. If tensions escalate, you may need professional family counseling, which can be extremely beneficial in helping you to move forward.

The grief journey is not one you take alone; with the help of God, family and friends, you can survive this very difficult season. Your marriage can survive and even be strengthened; your children can recover and grow as well. In the tumultuous ocean that is grief, cling to the life-raft of God's presence and promise.

My Wife

Beautiful, strong, smiling, engaging
until rogue waves of grief crash and
smash her onto the jagged rocks of despair.

Isolated, weakened and
disfigured by sorrow
battered and tortured before my eyes.

Slowly she rises until the next wave
crushes, batters and ravages
with its blunt-force anguish.

I watch helplessly as an ocean of grief has its way with her.

Eyes and Ears

My wife is tormented by grief
her face is etched by anguish
her breathing is labored
her sorrowful sighs reverberate
throughout the house.

I want to gouge my eyes out
and pierce my eardrums
become blind
to the disfigurement of grief
deaf
to her tormented groans.

her pain is excruciating
her wound swallows up everything in sight.

Let Me Out

The remaining children hear
"be careful," more often.

Their freedom
to come and go
is severely curtailed.

Their home
has become a place of
perpetual parental weeping.

Their mother and father
ravaged by sorrow.

Their home is no longer a refuge
but a den of despair.

Their desire for escape grows
but grieving parents want children close at hand
to touch, to see, to keep safe.
Tensions mount.

CHAPTER TWENTY-TWO

FORGIVING OR EXCUSING

Grieving puts you in a vulnerable state; you become naturally self-absorbed and easily wounded. While in this fragile condition, it is likely that you are or will be hurt, raising an important question—Do I need to forgive someone or excuse their actions? It's important to distinguish between the two: forgiveness flows out of an injustice, a wrongful act for which someone was responsible. In my personal experience, the ones who hurt me did so unknowingly. I needed to acknowledge their limitations and excuse their actions. Forgiveness may at times be appropriate, but often relationships simply need one or both parties to let things go. In both cases, forgiveness and excusing, the action is not just a single act, but is more of a process.

When our son died, forgiveness of others was not the main issue. Two people involved felt guilt, and we expressed our forgiveness to both them—to the driver of the vehicle, and also to a friend of Nathan's who was present with him just prior to the accident—but we never really thought either one was responsible for his death. The person we needed to forgive was Nathan, who had made a series of irresponsible decisions that ended in tragedy.

Instead of those who expressed guilt, the people who really hurt us were well-meaning supporters who made some thoughtless, insensitive statements. Their faith had been shaken, their image of God shattered. Rather than process what was happening, they chose to try to explain away our situation, to try to make sense of it, to inanely reference Bible verses.

The death of your loved one may have been the result of illegal activity, evil or neglect, caused by someone's deliberate actions or the intended or unintended results of those actions. Such actions or choices require forgiveness. Much has been written concerning forgiveness, so I simply want to mention a few particulars:

- It is important to forgive.

- "Unforgiveness does not stop the pain. It spreads it. Unforgiveness makes other people miserable.... It fouls relationships with complaints, bitterness, selfishness and revenge."[10]

- "Not forgiving someone is like drinking poison and expecting the other person to die."[11]

- Forgiveness does not excuse someone, but rather, it holds them accountable and names what they did as wrong!

- Forgiveness is a process that begins with the desire for the desire to forgive. God has forgiven you, and your ability to forgive and to even desire the desire to forgive, flows out of God's forgiveness, lived out in reality.

- Forgiveness does not mean the person is not held legally responsible, nor that there will be reconciliation of a prior relationship, if one existed.

- Forgiveness is a process through which we let go of hatred, anger, desire for revenge and begin to entrust that person to God. It takes time, but if you are on the pathway, you are forgiving.

So, back to the question above: it is important to differentiate between those you need to seek to understand and excuse, and those you need to forgive. Ask God and trusted companions to help you think through these two categories; even seeking counsel is a step on the pathway of forgiveness.

In my situation, the people involved were victims themselves; I needed to graciously excuse them for their ignorance and try to understand their motives. Both forgiveness and understanding can be difficult. It's important to keep in mind the fact that the process of forgiveness is not an event, and forgiving is often more about your own well-being than it is about the actions of another.

Angry Questions

What were you doing?
What were you thinking?
    My anger rages deep within
And I scream out a litany of questions:
Why, Nathan? Why?
Why were you up so late?
Why did you smoke marijuana?

---

10. Sittser, pages 140-141.
11. Wise saying of unknown origin.

Why did you leave the safety of your room?
Why were you on that roadway?
What were you doing?
What were you thinking?
Why, Nathan?
Why?

It makes no sense
It's so out of character
I do not understand

Why, Nathan, why?
I miss you so much
Your death is so tragic
so senseless

What were you doing?
What were you thinking?

You are gone
Taken from my life in a moment

Why, Nathan? Why?
What were you doing?
What were you thinking?

Asking for Forgiveness

Because of the tendency toward self-absorption, the need to care for yourself (placing the oxygen mask on your own face before you help others) and the uniqueness of grieving, at some point you will want to explore the question of whether you need to ask forgiveness from the members of your own family that may have been hurt by your actions or non-actions during this time. This is not a now thing, but it is something worth naming and being open to in the months to come.

CHAPTER TWENTY-THREE

ACCEPTANCE AND HOPE

Over time, God will prepare you to accept your new reality. Your willingness to be open and honest about your experience with yourself, God and others, to acknowledge and share your feelings, allows God to work in your heart and gradually give you a sense of peace. You may not notice the seedlings of acceptance breaking through the soil of your life, but your trusted companions, who are looking for any sign of healing, will be able to thank God for a hopeful future.

This eventual acceptance does not mean a pervasive happiness. You will likely continue to deal with the rogue waves of grief for the rest of your life, but the frequency and intensity will decrease. Acceptance doesn't mean you return to your previous normal; it is just the beginning of life on the other side of grief. You will be able to look ahead and make plans. When you see a photo or think about your loved one, you will not always be overwhelmed by sadness and may even experience joy, and feel gratitude for your memories. Sadness will still be present, but you will hear yourself sharing more openly and realistically about your loved one, often with a smile. The person you loved will not be identified by death alone, but also, even more often, by your life together.

How Are You

"I am alive and I got out of bed today,"
has evolved into
"Okay."
Something is happening.

The Sun

The sun is beginning to rise
*   illuminating the new landscape of my life.*

As it shines brighter,
    I notice profound changes in the
    geography of my heart.
The raging sea of sadness
    calms.
    Islands of joy emerge from the depths.
Along pathways of sorrow, flowers bloom.
    Vibrant colors of love, grace and mercy
    invite me to stop and enjoy their fragrances.
The rolling hills of despair
    sprout green patches of hope.
The harsh terrain is softening.
    The bleakness of this place has become
    less stark.
    Color and life have found their way here.

My life will be lived from a place forever changed—
    a place surrounded by a sea of sadness.
But as sure as the sun shines,
    it will also be a place where
    love, faith and hope
grow and flourish once again.

Chapter Twenty-Four

Take Care of Yourself

During grief, it is especially important to avoid isolation and personal neglect. The morose nature of depression tends to steal space and time that could be used for healing, for gratitude, for memories, for the living. You can intentionally take action that directs you toward God and life.

1. Be nice to yourself: consider your needs and what brings you joy and solace. Seek out life-giving distractions. Rest, eat well (even if you aren't hungry), and exercise (even if you don't feel like it).

2. Daily recall something for which you are grateful.

3. Take a walk alone or with friend. Both getting out of the house and being active will be beneficial.

4. Go out to breakfast/lunch/dinner/coffee/a movie with a trusted friend.

5. Get creative; try making a collage. Assemble some magazines from which to tear out words and pictures, and use a glue-stick to adhere them to paper. You may be surprised by what develops.

Exercises

The following processing techniques can be helpful tools for reflection. In order to get started, you will need paper and some writing instruments: pens, colored pencils, markers. Take your time, reflecting on and pondering the material, noticing what stirs within. I suggest you spend some time with one particular exercise, then break before returning to it a second time. Taking a pause can help you gain a new perspective or a deeper level of contemplation. There is no need to rush. The point is less about answering the questions, more about being in touch with your feelings and with God.

1. Meditate on John 11:33-35, especially the words, "Jesus wept." Jesus weeps for Lazarus, even though in a matter of moments, he will raise Lazarus from the dead. Imagine Jesus walking over to the tomb of his friend. The scripture tells us, "He was deeply moved in spirit and troubled" (v. 33b), "Jesus wept" (v. 35) and "Jesus, once more deeply moved, came to the tomb" (v. 38a). In all three passages, Jesus is emotionally expressive—deeply moved—by the death of his dear friend. Jesus understands your pain and knows you; honestly share your hurt with Jesus, knowing he loves you and weeps with you.

2. Verbalize your anger to God. Usually anger is not seen as a positive by Christians, yet Jesus was angry, the Psalmists were angry. Anger is a by-product of living in a broken world, and is often rightfully present in grief. If you are angry, honestly share your emotion with God. Remember, God desires our honesty. As you bring your anger to light and express it to God, it will lose some of its power over you.

3. Write a letter to God concerning your anger and/or other feelings which need to be expressed, to be released to God. After you write the letter, imagine yourself handing it to Jesus. Watch as he reads it. What do you see, feel, sense as Jesus reads your words? When he is finished, what does he do? Does Jesus come to you, speak to you? What do you see in his eyes? Take some time to sit with the one who loves you, is with you, cares about you, weeps with you.

4. Break some eggs. This elemental exercise can bring release on a number of levels. If you have one, smash eggs in your bathtub, where the mess is contained. They might splatter some, but it's worth it. You may wish to write words on the eggs, thereby combatting the lies that haunt you. See the egg-breaking as a prayer, a turning over of feelings and thoughts to God.

5. Slowly strip the petals off a flower, sharing your feelings with God as you process. Take time to notice the flower, feel the tug of removing a petal; as it is being stripped away, drink in its fragile beauty. Is there any hope or beauty after your loss?

6. Light a candle each night to remember your loved one, making sure you extinguish it before going to bed. When you light the candle, let it be a reminder of the light that shined through this person in life. When you blow it out, surrender your loved one to Jesus.

7. Are you feeling far from God? Write your own lament, sharing with God your honest doubts, frustrations, anger and sorrow. The Psalmists often expressed feelings of abandonment, but the truth is God never forsakes or forgets us. The

Psalmists were describing their emotions, not how things actually were. Read Psalms 42, 43, 73, 77, or 88. The Psalmists were expressing some of their most painful experiences in their poetic prayers, but they remained in conversation with God. Share your heart with unedited honesty.

Jeremiah wrote about his suffering in Lamentations. Use the examples below to help you share your deepest feelings with God.

> For these things I weep;
> My eye, my eye overflows with water;
> Because the comforter, who should restore my life,
> Is far from me.
> My children are desolate
> Because the enemy has prevailed (Lamentations 1:16, NKJV).

> See, O Lord, that I am in distress;
> My soul is troubled;
> My heart is overturned within me… (Lamentations 1:20a, NKJV).

> He has caused my flesh and my skin to waste away,
> He has broken my bones.
> He has besieged and encompassed me with bitterness and hardship.
> In dark places He has made me dwell,
> Like those who have long been dead.
> He has walled me in so that I cannot go out;
> He has made my chain heavy.
> Even when I cry out and call for help.
> He shuts out my prayer (Lamentations 3:4-8, NASB).

8. Slowly read the personal complaint Psalms—13, 35 and 86—and choose one with which to interact. Pay attention to the words or phrases to which you are drawn or resistant. Ponder them. How is God inviting you, reminding you, challenging, or encouraging you?

9. Create a collage, painting, or mixed media expression of your psalm.

CHAPTER TWENTY-FIVE

GUIDED MEDITATION

This form of meditation is best experienced through the guidance of another person, a spiritual director or trusted friend, but can also be accomplished by a recording of the prompts.[12] The point is to let another direct you, as you give your loss, pain and emotions to Jesus. You might want to repeat this meditation a few times during the first year.

- Get into a comfortable position, either in your favorite chair or on the floor.

- Begin to slowly, deeply breathe in and out, feeling your chest rise with each inhale and sink with each exhale. Let each breath remind you that God is the breath of life.

- Ask God to guide and direct you through this time, as you open your heart to what God has for you.

- Now, bring your loss to heart and mind.

- Allow yourself to feel all you are currently experiencing, every emotion stirring within you.

- Take all that you are feeling—pain, anger, fear, confusion, frustration, sorrow, despair—and place the feelings in a box of your own choosing. Notice the size of the box, its shape and color; see yourself lifting each emotion and placing it in the box one by one. Notice the weight as you lift it and place it in the box. When the box is filled, put the lid on it and imagine yourself sitting at a table with your box.

- Now imagine Jesus walking into your room and sitting down across from you. Jesus looks at you, looks deep within you. What do you feel as Jesus looks at you?

- Next, Jesus looks at your box. What do you feel as you see him eyeing your box?

---

12. For your convenience, we've made a recording of this meditation, which can be found at http://www.b-ing. org/, under the *Journey with Grief* tab.

- Jesus asks you, "What's in your box?" As you hear his question, what feelings are stirred within? Sit with your feelings before answering Jesus. What do you say to him? How do you feel as you share your response with him? What is his response to you?

- Jesus asks, "May I look into your box and examine its contents?" What feelings does his question stir up within you? Sit with your feelings.

- How do you respond to Jesus' request? As you respond, what feelings are stirring within you?

- Do you give Jesus the box? Why or why not?

- If you are not able to give Jesus your box, what is his reaction? What do his eyes communicate to you? Jesus rises and walks behind you. Gently placing his hands on your shoulders, he bends down to put his mouth next to your ear. What does he say to you? What are you feeling in response to his words?

- If you have chosen to give Jesus your box, what is his reaction? As you watch him open your box, what are you feeling? What is Jesus' reaction, as he explores the feelings you have placed within? What does he do with the contents of your box? What are you feeling as you watch this scene unfold?

- (For those of you who chose to give Jesus your box.) After Jesus is finished with your box, he slowly rises and walks behind you. Gently placing his hands on your shoulders, he bends down to put his mouth next to your ear. What does he say to you? What are you feeling in response to his words?

- Spend some time journaling about your experience, paying attention to any feelings that surface.

Chapter Twenty-Six

Benefits of Grieving

It is better to go to a house of mourning
than to go to a house of feasting,
for death is the destiny of everyone;
the living should take this to heart (Ecclesiastes 7:2).

Although not guaranteed, definite benefits can result from embracing the journey with grief. It is my prayer for you that honestly processing your experiences with God and with others will grow and deepen your faith, and, as your image of God is challenged and expanded, you will again trust in the mystery of the ever-changing, unchangeable one, God Almighty. I pray:

- Your compassion for others is increased. You are more able to be a comforting, non-anxious presence, trusting God and the process (see 2 Corinthians 1:3-7).

- You become more comfortable with mystery, more able to be open to God in the midst of the messiness and unpredictability of a broken world.

- You are more comfortable living with questions and less trusting of dualistic, black-and-white thinking; able to embrace the both/and realities of God and life.

- Your definition and awareness of the height, depth, breadth, and width of God's love is expanded.

- You have a new assurance that nothing can separate us from God's love; in the midst of grief, you have felt God's presence.

- You are more understanding of God and others, less quick to judge and more able to seek, listen and understand.

- You have a deeper appreciation of and stronger dependence on the eternal, the unseen, rather than depending on and trusting in the things that are seen. An enduring hope is born of this trust.

- You learn the value of honesty with God and attentiveness to your feelings.

- You begin to be more comfortable with yourself and with God.

- You begin to trust in the God of the fishes and the loaves, the "I can work with that" God.

- You gain a greater awareness of feelings, interactions and circumstances that are taking you toward God or away from God, and are able to adjust your mindset accordingly.

- You realize the importance of community and the need to be a safe presence for others.

If you would like to read about the long-term impact of my journey with grief on my life, go to the epilogue on page 152. There you will find my reflections on God and life some fifteen years after the death of my son, Nathan. This journey is not an easy one, but remember: you are not alone—God is with you, God is faithful and God can and does bring good out of every situation.

SECTION TWO

FOR YOU WHO JOURNEY WITH OTHERS

CHAPTER ONE

INSIGHTS FOR THE JOURNEY

In my experience, the Church is not always a place of safety and healing. My opinions and admonitions regarding grief and the grieving process are rooted in my own painful experience, as well as my observation of the suffering of others—suffering inflicted by well-meaning, but ill-prepared "care-givers." It may be hard to hear, but I know people who have left the Church because of the wounding words of others, spoken at an extremely vulnerable time. A journey through grief is a minefield, and even the most compassionate among us can be tripped up by good intentions. But it does not have to be this way. We can learn how to be the Church, to come alongside others, prepared to care well.

This section is not a detailed manual outlining the steps to success, a guarantee that your grieving friend or relative will experience your presence as life-giving and helpful. Each person and each person's journey with grief is unique. There are no guarantees. Rather, I am attempting to re-enforce a biblical foundation that will help you be a peaceful, non-anxious presence in your loved one's life, open to and responsive to the feelings and nuances of the situation and the person to whom you are attending, and attentive to God for wisdom and guidance. I also hope you gain some practical insights regarding care-giving, both intimately and from afar, for those who are suffering.

As you read, pay attention to the thoughts to which you are drawn and also those that cause resistance, taking time to explore each. You will discover areas for which you are naturally gifted, as well as areas that may require work. All is helpful to know, since awareness is the first step toward growth.

It is my hope and desire that God will use my shared experience to better equip you and the Church as sources of compassion, care and healing, to be instruments of God's love, grace and presence for those who are walking with grief.

Chapter Two

You Matter

Precious Friend

I love you my friend.

Your presence has been a gift from God
your touch
 tender and nurturing
your eyes
 compassionate and caring
your silence
 warm and inviting
your stillness
 safe and loving.

You have held
 my words
 my heart
 my soul.

You have carried
 my pain
 my sorrow
 my anguish.

You have allowed my wounds
 to wound you.

You have been
 present
 thoughtful
 concerned.

Thank you
You have been Jesus to me.

Coming alongside someone who is grieving can feel about as helpful as being a vase of flowers next to a hospital bed, but like those flowers, a grief companion is a beautiful presence that communicates love. Yet unlike those flowers, you, fully present, can listen, feel, embrace and be with—be Jesus to the person who is suffering. As I reflected on the safe people who were with me in my journey with grief, I wrote the poem above.

You have an important role to play in the unfolding grief journey of another. It is universally accepted that those who are grieving have both a strong urge to isolate, as well as a deep need for safe companions for the grief journey. (Safe companions in this context are trustworthy, sensitive, non-prescriptive, selfless, loving, empowered and led by God.) These dual realities—the tendency to withdraw and the need for others—highlight the importance of coming alongside a grieving person prepared to care in helpful ways. If one who has intimate access turns out to not be safe, the resulting hurt may push the grieving person further into isolation and away from potential sources of comfort, care and healing. Thus it is important for you to be a safe person and that is the focus and goal of this entire section of the book.

As you journey with another, remember the gift you bring to this sacred space is you—your ministry of presence. This internal acknowledgement of the importance of your presence to the grieving process will help you stay grounded in love and grace, and not succumb to waves of doubt, insecurity or the need to justify your place. Often the doubts and feelings of insecurity give birth to the actions and words that cause additional pain to those who are suffering, even when you enter with the best of intentions.

Journeying with someone who is suffering will likely be demanding and fraught with the unknown. It calls for ongoing vigilance, internal awareness (What am I feeling?), external awareness (What is the other person experiencing?) and God awareness (What is God doing? How is God leading me?). Yet your presence is extremely helpful and absolutely necessary. I leave you with the words of Jesus and Paul, each of whom deeply loved and trusted God, but longed for comfort from someone with flesh, someone who knew and cared about them.

Paul writes concerning the source of his comfort, "But God, who comforts the downcast, comforted us by the *coming of Titus...*" (2 Corinthians 7:6, emphasis mine).

And in the gospels, we read that in a time of suffering, Jesus choose to not be alone but to invite three others to be with him at a difficult time.

Then Jesus went with his disciples to a place called Gethsemane, and he said to them, "Sit here while I go over there and pray." *He took Peter and the two sons of Zebedee along with him*, and he began to be sorrowful and troubled. Then he said to them, "My soul is overwhelmed with sorrow to the point of death. Stay here and keep watch with me" (Matthew 26:36-38, emphasis mine).

Both Jesus and Paul knew the importance of people as a source of God's comforting presence and if the Son of God wanted his friends with him in a time of sorrow, then your friend likely desires and needs companionship too. You have an important role in the life of someone who is grieving, so take the time to interact and process through the following chapters so you are ready and able to flesh out the comforting love, care and presence of God to another.

REFLECTION

When you read about the importance and power of presence, the act of being Jesus to those who are suffering, what feelings and concerns arise within you?

Ask yourself the following questions:

- What am I feeling? (This is internal awareness.)
- What is the other person experiencing? (This is external awareness.)
- What is God doing? How is God leading me? (This is God-awareness.)

Which of these questions are you most comfortable with? Which are you the least comfortable with? Why?

Chapter Three

What You Don't Know

As you consider coming alongside one who is grieving, it is important to acknowledge that you have no idea what the other person is feeling/going through. You may think you do, especially if you have suffered a similar loss, but the grief experience is different for each person. The person's family system, faith, emotional capacity, personality, psychological make-up and temperament are unique, as are the circumstances surrounding the death. This uniqueness can show up in the cause of death (e.g., illness or accident), the suddenness of the death, the closeness of relationship with the person who died, whether violence was involved, whether suicide was involved—each of these things, and many others, have an impact on the experience of the person grieving.

Nicholas Wolterstorff, whose son died at age 25, noting the pain of loss, wrote:

> Death is the great leveler, so our writers have always told us. Of course they are right. But they have neglected to mention the uniqueness of each death—and the solitude of suffering which accompanies that uniqueness. We say, "I know what you are feeling." But we don't.[13]

And,

> Each person's suffering has its own quality. No outsider can ever fully enter in.[14]

This uniqueness means that you cannot come in with a set agenda and well-rehearsed monologue but rather need to be with the person in the moment, choosing to enter into this fluid time of fleeting feelings that are as powerfully overwhelming as they are unpredictable. Be open and aware, ready to weep or laugh, whatever the circumstances dictate, listening and being with the person while trusting God to lead and guide you through the encounter.

---

13. Wolterstorff, page 25.
14. Wolterstorff, page 72.

A Word to Those Who Have Suffered Loss

If you have suffered the loss of a loved one, please resist the temptation to think you know what the person is feeling and to compare your loss with theirs. Wherever you are on the spectrum of pain, and even if you are sharing with the hope of providing solace, comparison is not helpful.

In fact, comparison often leads to the minimizing of pain by the one comparing. It can unintentionally push the hurting person into taking over the role of comforter, or else cause the hurting person to push back against the comparing/minimizing. Either way, the good that was intended does not happen and, in fact, the exchange can cause additional hurt and drive the grieving person further into isolation.

Don't Compare

Let's resist the temptation to compare
our own grief with that of another.
Let's not minimize the pain of loss
especially our own.

Let's sit in sadness and silence
with one another
holding our grief as well as the other's.

Let's resist the temptation to compare.

Let's be with,
hold the other—
holding ourselves.

Now, although it is not helpful to compare, it is important to affirm that there is a very real bond that exists between those who have suffered loss and those who have recently lost a loved one. Those individuals who have entered into their grief openly and honestly, facing and dealing with their feelings, pain and questions, and interacting with God rather than seeking to escape, have an important gift to offer someone who is hurting. While you must understand that you cannot know exactly what another person is feeling, as one who has suffered and interacted with loss yourself, you can be a very powerful and helpful presence to the person journeying with grief.

Silent Kin

Within moments of meeting
the unspoken connection is known.
Communicated not by a secret handshake
but by sad eyes and
the knowing silence
a trembling embrace.
They too know the deep sorrow of loss.
They are our sisters and brothers in grief
present with us and to us
beyond words.

KNOWINGS FOR THE JOURNEY

Earlier in this chapter I stressed the importance of your role, and now I am affirming the importance of acknowledging that you do not fully know what a suffering person is dealing with, nor how you might best love and care for them. These twin truths—the importance of your role and the uniqueness of another person's journey—help foster a necessary dependence on God. God alone is all-knowing. God alone can impart the wisdom and insight necessary to journey with another in ways that communicate love, care and grace. The following chapters help lay the foundation that enables you to do just that.

REFLECTION

When you name and own the fact that you do not fully know what a suffering person is dealing with, nor how you might best love and care for them, what feelings surface within you?

Given the unknown realities associated with journeying with someone who is grieving, how do you resist the temptation to develop a comprehensive plan so that you may feel more comfortable in the interactions?

CHAPTER FOUR

GRIEF INSIGHTS

Moving On

No going back
no getting over it
only moving on
   forever changed
   forever wounded
moving on
   accepting the new reality
   navigating the new normal
moving on
   wearing pain and sadness
   living my worst nightmare
   come true

Before going any further, I want to make some general observations about the grief process and its various aspects, so you can have a sense of what is normal, beneficial or possibly hurtful. An expanded awareness can help you come alongside another, alert to possible danger signs and the unhelpful ways people deal with grief. Remember, the loss of a loved one changes everything.

Grief is a normal response to loss, not a source of shame or something to be pushed aside. Grieving is not a disease to be cured but a reality to be embraced. It's actually a pathway to becoming compassionate, gracious and caring. As someone is comforted in grief, they are enabled to come alongside others in the future. It's also an invitation to know and experience God, others and ourselves in new and deeper ways, an opportunity to uncover, expose and expand our image of God.

General Time Frames

No road map, no accurate or comprehensive articulation of the stages of grief exists, but a few general markers with some level of statistical verification can serve as time frame predictors. However, all time expectations are to be held loosely. See them as landmarks, not street signs; helpful, but not dependable.

After two or three months, subtle changes may be noticeable for some, but more likely the changes will begin about six months out; the physical manifestations of shock and despair are still present, but no longer debilitating. If after six months these behaviors remain intense, you may be witnessing Prolonged Grief Disorder, and the individual should be strongly encouraged to get professional help. It is estimated that about 10-15% fall into this category.[15]

The grief experience is unique to each person. There is not only one way to grieve or a "right" way to grieve. Grief is neither linear nor systematic, however, there are common elements to grief. When one is in the grip of grief, there is often a tendency to isolate from others, and this inclination can be intensified through painful interactions or insensitive conversations.

A companion on the grief journey would benefit greatly from a map with a "You Are Here" indicator and a layout of what lies ahead. The stages of grief model (denial, anger, bargaining, depression and acceptance) developed by Kübler-Ross provides at least some direction in the wilderness. That said, there is no longer universal agreement regarding the number or composition of the stages. If you are drawn to such schemas, hold them loosely, while keeping in mind a number of caveats: 1) the stages are not linear; 2) not everyone goes through all of them, or, if they do, not necessarily in the order in which they normally appear; 3) the so-called stages/steps can be repeated over and over—moving "forward" and then "back" again. The stages, although helpful descriptions, are not definitive and should not be overly relied on.

---

15. Some of this information is drawn from pages 14 and 109 of Ruth Davis Konigsberg's *The Truth About Grief*.

As you journey with another through grief, it is important to remember:

- Grief is a result of tectonic shifting in a person's life, and consequently is enormously unsettling, destabilizing and disorientating.

- Grief's impact is holistic (physical, cognitive, behavioral, social, spiritual, philosophical).

- Grief is a natural, God-given response to loss. Jesus grieved!

- Grief is an expression of love.

- ' Grief is not the final word.

- Each person's grief is unique.

- Grief is not linear—one may traverse the same geography of grief over and over again.

- Grief in some form will likely be a lifelong companion.

- There is no road map or blueprint for grief.

- There is no time frame for grief.

- There is no one way (right way) to grieve.

- There is no returning to what was, but only an open door into what is and will be.

- Even here God is at work!

TWO PHASES OF JOURNEYING WITH GRIEF

Your loving, caring, non-anxious and non-judging presence can help a person choose to feel and express what they are feeling and to embark on their unique journey with grief. As you come alongside another without judgment, you are:

1. Giving permission for the person to feel, name, experience what is going on within. This helps you to discover if the person is willing to journey with grief.

This is a critical choice that the one suffering will hopefully make. Your friend may think that honestly feeling what they are feeling is being a poor witness and dishonoring God, but your non-anxious, non-judging presence can help dissuade this type of thinking and free them to grieve.

Now that they are freed to freely grieve, they are ready to:

2. Choose to journey with grief. This choice flows out of the first choice to enter their grief and is the pathway to growth and transformation.

Once again, your presence can help them move forward with their grief—continuing to process what they are feeling; experiencing and sharing it with you and God. This all reinforces what was covered in Chapter Two—you matter.

TWO MANIFESTATIONS OF GRIEF

As an individual enters into their journey with grief, they tend to have two focuses:

1. Focus on the loss: Initially the reality of the loss eclipses all else, at least for a few days, weeks and even months. Practical acts of love and care are invaluable during this initial time—encouragement to eat, to rest and to not make major decisions are extremely helpful.

2. Focus on the future without the one who is gone. This prospect brings its own pain and continues to reoccur as the person realizes new losses, new never-to-be's, or never-again's. When Nathan died, the realizations of what would not be came unexpectedly out of nowhere, each one a sucker punch to the gut. Your presence can be very helpful at this point—a being with.

The above manifestations of grief are not mutually exclusive but likely, at some point, to happen in concert with one another. This can be enormously debilitating.

Price Tag

Death's price tag grows and grows
hopes
dreams
expectations
once held
surface only to be shattered
on the jagged rocks of death
    no college graduation
    no wedding
    no adult relationship
    no holidays together
    no Nathan
the cost climbs higher
with each realization

BARRIERS AND MISUNDERSTANDING

Some people who suffer the loss of a loved one will try to deny the grieving process. With knowledge, you can help move a person through the particular barrier they face, thereby providing freedom to heal and move on. If you are prepared, God can powerfully use you to speak truth into a shattered life. Your presence and gentle invitation to process can be just the encouragement needed (see page 128).

Below are some of the causes of impaired grieving:

1. Family history (e.g., feeling unimportant; having been brought up to look for the positive).

2. Dishonest view of emotions (i.e., a determination to have no anger or other negative emotions, especially toward God).

3. Fear of losing control ("If I let myself feel, it will overwhelm me").

4. Fear of pain ("There is no escaping it").

5. Desire to be a "good" Christian witness.

6. Friends' timetable for sadness.

7. Self-imposed timetable for sadness.

8. Church community's failure to embrace the person in pain.

FEELINGS AND REALITIES ASSOCIATED WITH GRIEF:

- Shock
- Numbness
- Emptiness
- Loneliness
- Isolation
- Confusion
- Loss of concentration
- Loss of short-term memory
- Fear

- Anxiety
- Heart ache/heaviness
- Relief
- Guilt
- Shame
- Anger
- Hopelessness
- Bodily aching
- Insomnia
- Sadness
- Wholistic weariness
- Despair
- Hope
- Joy
- Peace

Although not an exhaustive list, these and other feelings/symptoms can be present all at the same time. Loss of concentration and memory specifically contribute to the difficulty of daily tasks and overwhelming craziness. Inability to complete even simple tasks is normal (commonly referred to as "grief brain"), so just identifying the normalcy of these symptoms can be amazingly helpful. I know it was for me.

REFLECTION

Read through the list on page 99, which goes through the important things to remember as you journey with another. Which three do you think are most important for you to remember? Why? Which three would be the most difficult for you to internally embrace and remember? Why do you find those three so difficult?

As you read through the feelings and realities associated with grief on pages 101–102, which three are you most comfortable with? Which three are you least comfortable with? Why?

CHAPTER FIVE

REGRETS AND ANGER

On the journey with grief, the grieving person will often come face-to-face with questions and regrets. Both can bring on despair, which in turn erupts into anger. Understanding this sequence and its unpredictability can enable you to help your loved one to explore these feelings and express them in helpful and healthy ways. Your ability to be with them in whatever they are feeling provides a safe environment for processing.

Anger

Just below the surface
co-mingled
with sadness and fear
lies my anger

Anger at myself
for should-haves
could-haves
for missed opportunities
to be present with
to be present to
too few words of love
too few words of encouragement

Anger at God
for a son taken too soon
for the pain that torments my family, friends and me
for the wound that will never be healed
for the sadness we will always carry

This can be a bit complex because some people may not feel angry while others may not feel the interior freedom to be angry. The first thing to do is not to assume that everyone will be angry or that if anger is not being expressed it is because they are not feeling the interior freedom to be angry. This is where you trust the ministry of presence (see page 128) wherein you are, by your compassionate, non-anxious presence, creating a space for the grieving person to freely express, feel and process without the need to edit.

REFLECTION

Are you comfortable expressing your anger to God? Why or why not?

Are you comfortable allowing another person to communicate anger to God, or to tell you about their anger towards God in your presence, without defending God or needing to try to assuage their anger?

Avoiding Suffering

As we have already noted, the grief process is normal and necessary, yet some people seek to escape it. The methods of coping, or avoiding reality, mentioned below can be dangerous and destructive, so it is important to pay attention and to possibly intervene if indicated.

- Denial, suppression of experience
- Quickly moving through grief, in an effort to get back to normal—a normal that no longer exists
- Busyness; no space to grieve genuinely
- Use of God and scripture as a spiritual narcotic
- Numbing activities, such as drinking, eating, other types of bingeing
- Isolation from others
- Retreating into a fantasy world of their own creation

If the person is choosing to sidestep or suppress grief, you may need to come alongside that individual seeking to speak the truth in love, filled with grace. This is a messy proposition and there is a likelihood that the person will lash out and/or distance themselves from you. It is helpful to speak with a trusted individual before taking such a step and it may be most helpful to encourage the person to seek out a pastor, spiritual director, or therapist to help them process their grief.

CHAPTER SIX

GRIEF AND THE FAMILY

If you are called to journey with a couple who has lost a child, you need to be aware of the enormous stress such pain inflicts on a marriage. As previously stated, the grieving process endured by each parent is unique and unpredictable. A spouse may be tempted to compare the depth or the pace of their grief with their spouse's grief—moving on too fast, becoming stuck, minimizing the loss—or to assign blame. Also since grief is unique and it is likely that the spouses will grieve differently, they can begin to subtly or not so subtly make judgments about the level of grieving, pain and heartache of their partner—feeling that their partner is not really grieving, not really feeling the depth of loss as they are. This can lead to a choice to isolate themselves from one another.

Also since grief is often experienced like waves in an ocean, appearing and disappearing without warning, there can be a desire to escape the presence of the partner who is currently experiencing waves of sadness by the one who is in a period of calm. The person in the calm, enjoying momentary relief, does not want to be drawn back into the waves of despair, so they withdraw emotionally, even physically, from the hurting spouse. This can be experienced as abandonment, driving a wedge between the spouses. It is important to remember that each person is a reminder to the other of what has happened, of what was.

These natural, human behaviors are not something to be fixed, buried or ignored, but to be aware of and prayerfully brought to God. These differences regarding how each person grieves can cause additional stress and pain in their relationship and in their family. Also, be aware that all of these tendencies will have implications and ramifications when it comes to dealing with special days (birthday, holidays, etc.).

At some point counseling may be needed, but you knowing and even naming this tendency for them, the tendency to compare, blame and separate, can help normalize their experience and reduce tensions and frustrations. They may be consciously or subconsciously aware of these feelings, but naming and acknowledging them can keep what they are feeling from becoming a destructive eruption.

Spouses

death's dirge plays deep within
causing us to dance to its melody
each dancing
a different dance
at different times
with different partners
partners named
pain
despair
anger
each in turn having its way with us
each capable of driving us

farther

farther

apart

The complexities of family grief are not limited to parents, as the remaining children can be lost in an emotional abyss. Adult friends and family surround the couple, but quite often the children are unattended, their questions unanswered, their emotional needs unmet. Grieving parents can be very unsettling for a child in need of stability and support, especially in the throes of their own loss. Parents often become overprotective, fearful of letting a child or teenager out of sight. I cannot overestimate the importance of providing counsel, emotional support and normalcy for surviving children in the wake of death.

Younger Brother

Each night tears bathe his pillow
His brother, his friend,
his roommate, his hero
ripped from his life
He has never known a single day without him
Now he faces a lifetime without him

REFLECTION

Drawing from the above material, what realities can increase the stress within marriages and families journeying with grief?

What role can you play in helping them minimize the destructive nature of these realities?

CHAPTER SEVEN

COMFORTERS OF JOB

Often when the friends of Job are mentioned, it is more of a cautionary tale than a useful example of what it means to be a helping presence to someone who is hurting.

In fact, God specifically mentions their incompetence at the end of the book of Job, "My wrath is kindled against you and against your two friends, because you have not spoken of Me what is right..." (Job 42:7b, NASB). But their response to Job's grief was not wholly bad. I want to point out how these individuals' initial response is a wonderful model of coming alongside a hurting friend, and then I want to take a look at where they went wrong. Note in the following passage how Job's friends exemplified concern, compassion and care by their response and presence.

> Now when Job's three friends heard of all this adversity that had come upon him, they came each one from his own place, Eliphaz the Temanite, Bildad the Shuhite and Zophar the Naamathite; and they made an appointment together to come to sympathize with him and comfort him. When they lifted up their eyes at a distance and did not recognize him, they raised their voices and wept. And each of them tore his robe and they threw dust over their heads toward the sky. Then they sat down on the ground with him for seven days and seven nights with no one speaking a word to him, for they saw that his pain was very great (Job 2:11-13 NASB).

PRINCIPLES LEARNED

1. These caring individuals were Job's friends. They had a relationship with him prior to his trials. Keep that in mind as you consider involving yourself in the life of someone who is hurting: examine first the level and nature of

your relationship with the person prior to this event. If your relationship was a close one, gently come alongside your friend in the natural way you have always related to one another. You will know. If, on the other hand, you were not particularly intimate, send a sympathetic note or a plant. Pray for them and for those who will be surrounding them at this time. Loving from afar in practical ways is an extremely helpful and powerful way to be Jesus to someone who is hurting (see page 142ff).

2. They heard. I interpret this to mean that the news grabbed them, touching their hearts and compelling them to go to their friend. They were moved by the news regarding the great losses of their dear friend.

3. They went. Dismissing their own plans, they went to be with him in his suffering, having no idea what they would find or what might be asked of them. They did not ask if there was something Job needed, which is rarely a helpful question in crisis, as the person in pain is often unaware of what's needed. Pain and sorrow dull the ability to process physical need, but these men chose to be with Job in his pain. This step of going to and engaging with the person hurting can be difficult—full of paralyzing fear and uncertainty. It is best to name all that you are feeling with God and seek to ground yourself in the foundational truths of scripture that help one to be present to and with another in healthy, healing ways (see page 126ff).

4. Their goal was to sympathize and comfort. I would even use the word empathize—to feel with, to enter into the reality—as it better communicates what they actually did. The word comfort is tricky; we often understand it as taking away pain, and that is not really possible nor is it always the best goal. Comfort can come through being with another in their sorrow. The simple presence of a trusted friend can be a reminder that God is with them, which can be a source of great comfort and the beginning of healing—the person is not alone. People in the midst of loss need "safe" companions. The importance of the ministry of presence, simply being with, cannot be emphasized enough (see page 128).

5. They saw that their friend was disfigured by his grief and reacted accordingly, raising their voices, weeping, tearing their robes and throwing dust on their heads. Job's grief became their grief. This is the definition of compassion—the choice to come alongside and suffer with one who is hurting.

6. They sat with him in silence. No one said a word for seven days. Having entered into their friend's pain, they could experience in a small way the

great pain he was enduring, and they knew no words were appropriate or welcome. At this point their presence, their entering into and identifying with the pain of their friend, was what was needed.

These six guiding principles, helpful for anyone considering walking with someone who is suffering, begin with having an established prior relationship with the person and acting in concert with the level of that prior relationship. Then, in the context of that relationship, you must be willing to enter into the painful reality of your friend's circumstance, refrain from offering words and be a loving, caring, comforting presence. It is important to determine if you have the type of relationship that gives you access into the life of the person who is suffering and determine, if so, whether you are equipped to journey with them.

WHAT WAS MISSING

So where did the friends go wrong, so wrong that God became angry with them? The breaking of the silence was actually Job's doing. He chose to share his heart, his unedited feelings with his friends. In his despair, he questioned the wisdom of God. Job ends his lament with the following words, "For sighing has become my daily food; my groans pour out like water. What I feared has come upon me; what I dreaded has happened to me. I have no peace, no quietness; I have no rest, but only turmoil" (Job 3:24-26).

Having heard Job cry in despair, these faithful friends, who have shared Job's pain, silently caring and comforting him by their presence, now feel compelled to speak. They begin to share their insights regarding why this has happened, defining and defending God, correcting and advising Job. This tendency to speak, to defend God, to advise and try to make sense of the situation, is difficult to resist, but rarely helpful and can be dangerous. Also note two other observations that may help one avoid going down that path: God actually gets angry with Job's friends because of their words, and Job, on his own, eventually emerges from his suffering and questioning of God with a deeper, more robust faith.

I'm not suggesting a comforter will never be in a position to speak, but because offering opinions and advice is often our default, this passage is a good reminder of the power of presence and the danger of words. We tend to feel self-conscious in silence, and our awkwardness can lead us to fill the space with words. Understanding that tendency, it is best to enter in committed to silence, quick to listen and slow to speak, and then discern what's helpful as time unfolds.

REFLECTION

Which of the above six principles is a strength for you? Why? Which might be an area that invites growth?

What steps might help you partner with God as you seek to grow in this area?

CHAPTER EIGHT

COUNTING THE COST

Visitor, Beware

Don't come to cheer me up.
Come to cry
to hold
to be with.

Don't come to cheer me up.
Come to embrace my pain
sadness
sorrow
loss.

Don't come to relieve my pain.
Come to be with me in the moment
ready to
listen
laugh
cry.

Come to enter in
or
don't come at all.

Coming alongside someone who is hurting can be a helpful, beautiful act of love, compassion and care, but you need to know that entering another person's pain-filled season won't be easy. This will not be a relationship of mutuality. Your time with this suffering person may leave you depleted, wrung out, done. Be prepared to sacrifice, to suffer, to be uncomfortable repeatedly. If you aren't aware of and prepared for the challenges ahead, you may be a casualty along the way.

First, know your limitations: don't underestimate the personal cost to you or your family. It is possible to get sucked into the swirling vortex of another's grief and be unable to extricate yourself from it (see page 126). Pay attention to the gravitational pull this has on you, remembering it is their story, and, though you are choosing to enter in, it is not yours to take on. God is using you but you are not the Savior, you are not God. Ultimately you must leave this person in God's care.

Secondly, as you journey with another, it is important to intentionally care for yourself. Take the time you need to be renewed and refreshed by life-giving activities. The discipline of self-care will enable you to continue as a positive presence, dependent on God to guide and direct your interactions. An ongoing awareness and processing with God and others is extremely helpful—what began as a good God-honoring effort does not guarantee a good God-honoring ending.

ℬ Referrals: Professional Help

Grief is a difficult journey with unique challenges. It can be very demanding and destabilizing for all involved, but others have walked this road before. Resources exist. As you journey with another, it is helpful to have a list of such resources you can provide the person who is grieving: names of therapists, grief support groups, pastoral counselors, spiritual directors, grief-related books (see page 157 for some book suggestions). Someone at your local church may be able to help, but if a list isn't readily available, begin to compile one.

Below I have listed nine difficulties associated with the journey with grief, some or all of which might help you discern the comforter role you may best be able to perform. The key is to be honest. These statements are designed to foster self-awareness and allow you to invite God into challenging spaces. Also keep in mind that your presence with the person is not the only helpful way to care for someone who is hurting (see page 142ff).

NINE POTENTIAL CHALLENGES AHEAD

1. An untested faith may leave you unprepared to personally journey with another through the valley of the shadow. Thankfully, many have not experienced suffering to the degree caused by the death of a loved one and have not had to navigate the accompanying issues of faith that often arise. Deep and profound suffering is a faith journey unto itself. Paul writes in 2 Corinthians 1:3-4, "Blessed be the God and Father of our Lord Jesus Christ, the Father of mercies and God of all comfort, who comforts us in all our affliction so that we will be able to comfort those who are in any affliction with the comfort with which we ourselves are comforted by God" (NASB).

2. Although Jesus spoke often of trouble and pain, you may have difficulty believing God can use suffering for good. The inability to grasp this difficult concept will tempt you to focus on rescuing the person, rather than simply walking alongside. The truth is that God can and does use suffering to expand one's capacity to channel love and grace, to shape an individual into a fuller Christlikeness. God is greater than suffering.

3. Your trust in God may be centered on God's provision and protection rather than in God's love and goodness, regardless of circumstances. A deliver-me-from-circumstances faith is not going to be sufficient in extreme despair. One needs to be grounded in the "enoughness" of God's goodness, power, love and grace, independent of life's circumstances. The passages shared on page 118 and following are helpful reminders of God's trustworthiness.

4. You may feel a need to defend God. If someone you care about is suffering it may seem to reflect negatively on God. Additionally, if the one in pain is actually lashing out at God, a natural tendency to defend God arises, as in the case of Job and his friends. Your trust in God's love, goodness and power must override your felt need to defend God (see #3 above).

5. Occasionally you may feel the need to fit adverse circumstances into an existing belief system regarding God, God's identity and God's behavior. A desire to make someone's difficult circumstances fit your image and identity of God changes the entire dynamic of the encounter. Instead of being a presence of comfort, the would-be comforters seek to make sense of the situation and bolster their own faith. My wife experienced such a painful relationship, as a well-meaning person sought to make sense of the loss of our child. After brief questioning, it suddenly made sense to this

person that God took our child because we had "so many."

6. Often a person feels the need to fix things, be helpful, or give advice. It is difficult to simply see someone in pain without addressing it some way, without trying to do something, anything that might alleviate the pain of the situation. This natural desire to resolve the situation must be resisted because it can cause devastating harm. Rather, it's important to simply be present and responsive to the person in need.

7. Many of us are uncomfortable with the suffering of others. Implicit in the role of comforter is the ability to be present with the suffering of another, to allow them to feel what they are feeling (anger, doubts, despair), and even to experience tears and unedited processing as a vulnerable, valuable gift. This ability to be with is a fruit of trusting in the person and character of God (see #3 above).

8. It's possible that the pain of another reminds you of your past pain or loss. You need to be aware of this possibility going in and guard yourself against becoming the one who needs comfort. I have experienced this role reversal and found it to be frustrating and exhausting.

9. Comforting another may be unsettling, as you realize this experience could be yours. The pain of another is a reminder that this world is broken; sorrow and loss are possible for anyone at any time. The fact that life is precarious can be extremely unsettling, and the anxiety caused by this realization may greatly hinder your ability to come alongside another.

The nine difficulties above are real dangers, which, if experienced in a way that shapes your interaction with one who is suffering, can cause them additional pain. In an effort to avoid further, unintentional pain, the suffering person may isolate even more, separating from the community that could be a wonderful source of ongoing care and healing. None of the above challenges are insurmountable, and none of us are fully immune to them. It is important to know ourselves, emotionally and spiritually, and to honestly assess our ability to offer the ministry of presence, always leaning on God for discernment, strength, wisdom and guidance along the way.

Stay Away

Please stay away

if you come out of duty
or want to explain
if you want to defend God
or make sense of my situation
if you want to entertain
or get me to smile

Please stay away

if you know why this happened
or want to regale me with stories of
heaven
if you view silence a void to fill
with words
or Bible verses

Please stay away

if you can't be with me in the moment
if you are unable to enter my grief and pain

send a plant
and by your discretion
you will have saved us both
much pain.

REFLECTION

Which three of the "Nine Potential Challenges" listed above do you feel like you have a good handle on? Why?

Which three of the "Nine Potential Challenges" listed above do you feel would be a personal challenge for you? Why?

CHAPTER NINE

BIBLICAL FOUNDATION

Before going further, I want to lay a biblical foundation for caregiving that will help you be with one who is suffering. Joshua 1 links together two words, *strong* and *courageous*, three separate times. The Hebrew word for *strong* denotes a strength that results from binding oneself to a more substantial something—like a sailor in a storm lashing himself to the mast. The sailor alone is not able to withstand the fury and power of the storm, but attached to the mast, he is! *Courageous* speaks of being resolute of mind, intently focused on something or someone. The three passages in Joshua 1 refer to three things on which one is to be focused: the promises of God (v. 6), the word of God (v. 7) and the person/presence of God (v. 9). The challenge and invitation is to bind yourself to God, to focus upon the promises, word and person of God prior to, during and following your time as a caregiver.

Your view of God and knowledge of God's love will definitely come into question. The following passages will help you stay strong, as you bind yourself to scripture and focus on the truth of God's character. These passages are for you, not for sharing with the person who is in pain; they are meant to support you in your walk, to provide a foundation that will help you remain a compassionate presence.

Ecclesiastes reminds us there is a time and place for grieving, and that grieving is not only normal, but can be used by God to bring perspective to life:

Ecclesiastes 3:1, 3b, 4 (NASB): There is an appointed time for everything. And there is a time for every event under heaven…a time to heal…A time to weep and a time to laugh; a time to mourn and a time to dance.

Ecclesiastes 7:2-4 (NASB): It is better to go to a house of mourning… because that is the end of every man, and the living takes it to heart.

Sorrow is better than laughter…The mind of the wise is in the house of mourning, While the mind of fools is in the house of pleasure.

As you enter into the house of mourning with another, it will be a sobering experience, a time to take stock of your beliefs about God, heaven, hope, your own life. Don't deny yourself time and space to process what is surfacing within you.

Paul writes in Romans 12:15, "Rejoice with those who rejoice, and weep with those who weep" (NASB). This passage is a reminder that you are not to set the agenda, but to respond to whatever the person is experiencing. This openness to the here-and-now flows from binding yourself to and focusing on the promises of God regarding suffering (comfort, growth, transformation, deepening faith), the word of God that speaks to God's abiding presence, love and faithfulness, to the hope we have now and to come in Christ Jesus, and the person of God with us.

AN ANCHOR FOR YOU

One familiar passage is meant for you alone, not to be shared with a person in the throes of grief: Romans 8:28, "And we know that in all things God works for the good of those who love him, who have been called according to his purpose." It is so helpful to own the truth that God can and will bring good out of this situation, not that the circumstance itself is good, but that only God can use it for good. I believe God will share this passage at the proper time with a grieving person who is gradually gaining perspective, hopefully beginning to heal, but no passage is more powerful for you in the midst of the storm.

Romans 8:26-27 brings me great solace as I journey with others: "In the same way the Spirit also helps our weakness; for we do not know how to pray as we should, but the Spirit Himself intercedes for us with groanings too deep for words; and He who searches the hearts knows what the mind of the Spirit is, because He intercedes for the saints according to the will of God" (NASB). Although they may not be able to pray or even want to pray, I know that the Holy Spirit is praying on their behalf, praying from the depths of their being. When appropriate, this can be a helpful passage to share with one who is struggling with prayer.

2 Timothy 2:13, which says, "If we are faithless, he remains faithful, for he cannot disown himself," can be helpful to you and to the person with whom you are journeying. It is a reminder that God is faithful—end of story! Also, if someone is struggling with their faith, this passage reminds us God is and will remain faithful, for they belong to God; it is impossible for God to not be faithful to them, to us.

Romans 8:38-39 says, "For I am convinced that neither death, nor life, nor angels, nor principalities, nor things present, nor things to come, nor powers, nor height, nor depth, nor any other created thing, will be able to separate us from the love of God, which is in Christ Jesus our Lord" (NASB).

Romans 8:1 says, "Therefore there is now no condemnation for those who are in Christ Jesus" (NASB).

The last two passages above are foundational for all of us. God's love cannot be thwarted by circumstances, no matter how horrific. God is still loving, and God's love is within and surrounding you and all who are involved in tragic circumstances. Secondly, there is no condemnation that originates with God. The truths in these passages can encourage the one who is grieving to come to God with unedited honesty and free you to be alongside in that honesty, owning God's unconditional love.

The scripture passages below remind us of the hope we have even in suffering; loss is not the final word. Although an anchor for your soul, these verses are not to be immediately shared with one who is grieving. For now, bind yourself to them and take refuge in God's promise for all believers. The hope you have enables you to be with someone else through suffering, not to eliminate pain, but to provide assurance of God's goodness and love. At some future point down the road, when the pain of loss is not as raw, God may lead you to share one or more of these words that affirm the hope that is ours, the hope that does not disappoint.

Blessed are those who mourn, for they will be comforted (Matthew 5:4).

The Lord is close to the brokenhearted and saves those who are crushed in spirit (Psalm 34:18).

Those who sow with tears will reap with songs of joy (Psalm 126:5).

He heals the brokenhearted and binds up their wounds (Psalm 147:3).

But we do not want you to be uninformed, brethren, about those who are asleep, so that you will not grieve as do the rest who have no hope (1 Thessalonians 4:13, NASB).

I consider that our present sufferings are not worth comparing with the glory that will be revealed in us (Romans 8:18).

Consider it pure joy, my brothers and sisters, whenever you face trials of many kinds, because you know that the testing of your faith produces perseverance. Let perseverance finish its work so that you may be mature and complete, not lacking anything (James 1:2-4).

He will wipe every tear from their eyes. There will be no more death or mourning or crying or pain, for the old order of things has passed away (Revelation 21:4).

Psalms

Inundated by
bumper sticker theology
and greeting card sentiments

I flee to the solace
the raw honesty
and naked emotions
of the Psalms.

HONESTY BEFORE GOD

The following passages are freedom-giving passages that encourage those who are suffering to express themselves to God with unedited honesty. (If anger with God makes you uncomfortable, take some extra time to consider the scriptures below.) These Psalms of Lament are responses to life crises, questioning God's trustworthiness to protect from injustice, chaos, and death. They also emphasize the with-ness, for-us-ness, faithfulness of God and free those who are suffering to approach God with unrestrained emotions, believing God is able to receive whatever they bring in their pain. These Lament (or Complaint) Psalms make up the largest number of Psalms—there are 67 of them—and that's not surprising, given that we live in a broken world, not yet fully redeemed by God.

The Imprecatory Psalms (see Psalms 58, 69, 109), named from the word "imprecate," which means "to pray evil against" or "to invoke curse upon" another, are Psalms that are raw in the extreme. They call down God's judgment on the psalmist's enemies and even the children of the enemies. They are so raw and angry that they can be a source of embarrassment, yet they are included in the Bible for their honest articulation and, in that brutal honesty, grant us permission to do the same.

I am worn out from my groaning. All night long I flood my bed with weeping and drench my couch with tears (Psalm 6:6).

My tears have been my food day and night, while people say to me all day long, "Where is your God?" (Psalm 42:3).

My heart is in anguish within me; the terrors of death have fallen on me (Psalm 55:4).

How long, O Lord? Will You forget me forever? How long will You hide Your face from me? How long shall I take counsel in my soul, Having sorrow in my heart all the day? (Psalm 13:1-2a, NASB).

I am benumbed and badly crushed; I groan because of the agitation of my heart (Psalm 38:8, NASB).

I am bowed down and brought very low; all day long I go about mourning. My back is filled with searing pain; there is no health in my body. I am feeble and utterly crushed; I groan in anguish of heart (Psalm 38:6-8).

My eyes are dim with grief. I call to you, Lord, every day; I spread out my hands to you (Psalm 88:9).

(The entirety of Psalm 88 is filled with unedited honesty.)

Be merciful to me, Lord, for I am in distress; my eyes grow weak with sorrow, my soul and body with grief. My life is consumed by anguish and my years by groaning; my strength fails because of my affliction, and my bones grow weak (Psalm 31:9-10).

Doubts, anger, confusion, questions, accusations—all emotions are allowed; all are welcome. God is not too delicate; God is not a God of illusion or facades. Our God is a down-and-dirty, in-the-trenches God, who desires and invites genuine, open interaction, always choosing honesty over dishonesty, no matter how well-intended denial or pretense may be.

These Psalms remind us to let people express themselves freely to God, while resisting the temptation to defend God or curtail honest proclamations, accusations, or frustrations. Remember Jesus' words in the garden, where he said, essentially, "I don't want to do this," and on the cross, where he asked, "Why have you forsaken me?" Jesus was brutally honest with God. So a person in the throes of grief must be allowed to be honest in your presence and before God. Although it may be challenging to hear, if you are able, create an opportunity for God to be present through you.

Walking with another is a journey filled with the unknown, filled with the need to be with God and another person in the moment. Emotions can be strong and when expressed, unsettling. It's so important to be grounded in and focused on something (God's promises) and someone (the Triune God). These focuses will provide the perspective needed for such a sacred and demanding undertaking.

The Offering

I come to God
with fists clenched
in rage

with a heart broken
by sorrow

with a life shattered
by loss

and these
are the very gifts
I offer to
God

for they are all
I have to give

REFLECTION

Which of the promises mentioned in the chapter above will you claim for yourself?

How comfortable are you with the expression of doubts, anger, and accusations regarding faith and God?

Are you able to be with another as they freely process? Be honest, because this can be extremely difficult, and there are other ways to demonstrate love (see page 142ff).

Chapter Ten

Jesus and Suffering

Isaiah 53 describes Jesus as "a man of sorrows, and acquainted with grief" (KJV). Like the psalmists, Jesus, fully human in his suffering, cried out to his Father with raw emotion. Jesus' freedom to be real before God flowed from knowing he was deeply loved by the Father, and nothing could change that. As a student of the Hebrew scriptures, he was familiar with the Psalms and likewise chose to openly express his feelings, unafraid of damaging his own testimony or making God look bad. We read in Psalm 62:8, "Trust in him at all times, you people; pour out your hearts to him, for God is our refuge." Jesus was free to fully pour out his heart because he trusted God. His example reminds us that grief is good and godly; it is also good and godly for those who are grieving to share openly and honestly with God.

Let's look at two specific examples of interaction between Jesus and God the Father.

The first instance is recorded in Luke 22:41-44. As the time of Jesus' death drew near, he retreated to the garden of Gethsemane to pray, taking with him three friends. (Although this is not the focus of this illustration, it is a good reminder of the importance of people being present with those who are grieving. Jesus chose three friends to be with him during this difficult time, a reminder of the need for and importance of the ministry of presence (see page 128). Sadly for Jesus, those he chose were not able to be with him as he desired.

The physician Luke describes the anguish Jesus felt as being so great that he sweated drops of blood. In his suffering, Jesus turned to God, asking if there was another way forward, apart from death on the cross. Not once, not twice, but three times Jesus asked to be released by his Father from his impending death. Jesus honestly communicated with God—he didn't say what he thought God wanted to hear, and he didn't merely accept what was going to take place. He chose to fervently share his desire with God without reservation or apology.

A second example occurred several hours later, as Jesus was hanging on the cross. In a moment of unedited honesty, Jesus cried out, "My God, my God, why have you forsaken me?" (Matthew 27:46b). These words are striking for two reasons: First, this is the only time Jesus ever addresses his Father as God. It's as if Jesus was expressing the extraordinary distance from God he felt at that moment. Secondly, this statement seems almost irresponsible. Jesus, who claimed to be the Messiah and more, and who also claimed to be God (throughout the gospel of John), declared that he felt forsaken by God. How is this even possible? Once again, Jesus was not hampered by fear of how people would interpret what he was saying. He was being honest with his Father, whom he addressed simply as God, while sharing the raw emotions of his heart.

This trust in God freely flows from the truths embodied by the life, death and resurrection of Jesus—the power and love of God. The cross and the empty tomb enable us to ignore the dubious voices and current circumstances, to continue to focus on the person of God as seen in the death and resurrection of Jesus.

Let's look briefly at the story of Jesus and the death of his close friend, Lazarus, recorded in John 11. Having received word that Lazarus had died, Jesus went to the tomb, where he saw others gathered and weeping. John tells us, "He was deeply moved in spirit and troubled" (11:33), "Jesus wept" (11:35), and "Jesus, once more deeply moved, came to the tomb" (11:38). In these three passages, Jesus is emotionally expressive regarding the death of his friend, even though he knew he would shortly be raising Lazarus from the grave. This is significant as you journey with someone suffering the loss of a loved one: although we know there is hope, sorrow is still felt. Jesus grieved the loss of his friend; Jesus wept; Jesus allowed himself to feel the sting of death. This story helps us understand and even encourage grieving—knowing that Jesus did the same and that we do not grieve as the world grieves, for we have hope in the goodness, grace and love of God and in God's power that overcame death.

REFLECTION

What can you take from the statements of Jesus in the garden and on the cross?

As you consider Jesus' emotions regarding the death of his friend, what stands out to you?

What insights can these passages provide as you come alongside others?

CHAPTER ELEVEN

FOUNDATIONAL TRUTHS

The following truths are important as you enter into the pain and suffering of another. Internalizing these will help you stay grounded and have access to necessary strength, wisdom and insight. Whether going through a difficult time yourself or walking with another, know these basics concerning God's presence and power in all circumstances. You may not fully embrace them all, but Jesus will hear and honor a simple prayer for more belief. Pay attention to the ones that evoke a heartfelt "yes" in you, as well as to those with which you need help. God can use you where you are and grow you from there.

1. God is already at work. Before you arrive, while you are present and after you leave, God is at work bringing good out of any situation, helping to heal and shape a person journeying with grief. This is not to say the circumstances are good, but rather that circumstances do not change God's goodness or identity, nor hinder God's ability to love, impart grace or make good out of any circumstances.

2. God's grace is present. Although not always evident, we are assured in the depth of our being that God is faithful, and God's grace is abundant. Remembering this truth about God can help you remain present to the person who is suffering and to God.

3. Love will win. God's love cannot and will not be defeated, and nothing can separate us from that love—not even death. God's love is the constant for all of us. It is the dependable safety net under the high-wire journey with grief. This love poured into your heart will flow out to another as you continue to lean on and yield to the presence and power of God.

4. God desires to use suffering and even tragic events to bring people to a deeper knowledge and awareness of God's identity and character. This is what happened to Job as he journeyed with God in and through suffering.

5. Learn to trust God beyond what you see, hear and touch. You likely will not know what God is doing, just as the disciples were unable to comprehend what Jesus was doing on the cross, but you do know that God is loving, powerful, compassionate and gracious. That is what you hold on to. Trust God and lean not on your own understanding.

6. We partner with God in God's work. God is at work, and your role is to be a partner in what God is doing, letting go of agendas, time frames and opinions. Trust God and trust God's process, as you seek to follow God's leading. It goes without saying that your ongoing, growing relationship with God is vitally important.

7. God will bring good out of any situation. Nothing can prevent it. God's love, grace and power cannot be neutralized by horrific actions or the catastrophic circumstances of life.

These seven foundational knowings can be boiled down to one thing: trusting God. Your trust in God enables you to experience shalom (Hebrew for "peace"), peace in spite of circumstances, not because of circumstances. Isaiah 26:3 says "You will keep in perfect peace those whose minds are steadfast, because they trust in you." To the degree that you are able to bind yourself to and stay focused on the person of God—the goodness, power, love and grace of God—the promises and word of God, you will have the peace that flows from God…peace that God is enough and you are enough.

Once again, there are no expectations that you fully internalize these truths, but a hope that you will identify with them and ask God to help you own them. Remember, God is the God of fish and loaves, the God who can do in and through you that which is beyond your ability to ask or imagine.

REFLECTION

Which of the above foundational truths have you internalized to such a degree that it has shaped you and your view of life?

Which of the above foundational truths do you find most challenging and why?

CHAPTER TWELVE

MINISTRY OF PRESENCE AND LISTENING

As stated earlier, willing listeners are enormously important on the journey with grief. Jesus brought friends with him to the garden and Paul received comfort through his companion, Titus. These examples affirm the importance of a person (you) coming alongside another in what I call the ministry of presence.

What Is Presence?

The ministry of presence involves the ability to be with and non-anxiously engage with another in the now of their experience, not seeking to control or take responsibility for what they are feeling, being comfortable with their tears, anger, silence and words, not needing to defend God nor fix nor reinterpret the felt reality of the person grieving—able to rejoice and weep—trusting and depending on God's leading and resources—manifesting love and compassion by your being with the person grieving and thus creating a safe place for them to be open and honest.

Your presence is an important source of comfort, healing, love and care—a reminder of the goodness of God during a time when the person grieving may feel very distant from God. You are Jesus with skin on, the real-time incarnation of God's love; this is true whether you are personally present or caring from a distance (see page 142ff).

🎶 Motivations

Awareness of your motivation to help is important, especially as the grief process lengthens. You can start off well, maintaining good boundaries, taking care of yourself, not taking on pain and responsibilities that are not yours to assume. However, over time it is easy to begin to over-appreciate the need to be needed or to take personal responsibility for the other's overall health.

It is important to regularly step back and ask God to help you discover what is fueling your efforts. Are you still being led by God, or is something else driving you? Be honest in your exploration; remember it is not about condemnation, but awareness. Your goal is to be a healthy, supportive, caring, giving presence, not one who brings additional pain and drama into the mix.

QUICK TO LISTEN

James 1:19b says, "But everyone must be quick to hear, slow to speak..." (NASB).

James' admonition could not be more spot on! If you remember, the comforters of Job (page 109ff) were a perfect example of godly companions when they kept silence, but as soon as they opened their mouths, the encounter started to go bad. Keep that story in mind as you enter into a ministry of presence. The same letters that make up the word *listen* can be rearranged to spell *silent*. It is your silence that gives you the best opportunity to truly listen—to God and to the one to whom you minister. When you resist the temptation to fill silence with words, you begin cultivating a safe, healing, permission-giving place for those who grieve. Within that safety, they are free to be honest.

Silent

Your wordless presence
Creates space for reflection
God's love shining through

ACTIVE LISTENING

I have used the word listening rather than hearing, even though the words are often interchangeable. While hearing naturally happens, listening, especially active listening, takes some concerted effort. Listening, beyond the physical hearing of words and seeking to understand what is communicated by the words, facial expressions, body language and tone.

Active listening involves an ongoing conscious decision to engage and concentrate, seeking to understand what is holistically being communicated. This type of listening takes energy and the skills used can take time, determination, practice and patience to hone. Active listening generates connection, fosters understanding, and cultivates trust as you create the space and time for the person to discover, explore, and name their thoughts and feelings.

Before getting into the nuts and bolts of active listening, let's explore the non-verbal indicators that communicate to another, *I am here, I care, I am listening*:

1. Nodding as the person is sharing.

2. Making eye contact, looking into a person's eyes (without staring).

3. Maintaining a posture that communicates engagement (leaning toward, facing the person).

4. Facial expressions that communicate you are tracking, concerned, sad.

These intentional actions take concentration, and ongoing engagement takes energy, so it is important to enter into these situations rested and ready for the work of active listening. If you are not intentional or have limited energy and internal space to be with another, you can easily slip into negative behaviors that communicate, *I am not present, I am not engaged or I don't/can't care*:

1. Fidgeting.

2. Looking at a clock or watch.

3. Doodling, playing with your hair or picking your fingernails.

These signs of distraction are not helpful and can even be experienced as hurtful, pushing the person toward greater isolation.

ACTIVE LISTENING SKILLS

The following behaviors can be developed over time, becoming natural and free-flowing. As you read through the list, ask yourself which one(s) might be helpful for you to begin to intentionally cultivate and then begin to practice in conversations with others.

1. Pay attention to your non-verbals (see above). This is ongoing.

2. Paraphrase what the person has shared, using your own words. This helps the person know you are hearing and understanding what they are saying. Discovering a misunderstanding opens the door for more dialog and clarification.

3. Use brief prompts to keep the conversation going and show you are listening: "Then?" "And?" This encourages the speaker to continue to share, communicating your interest and hopefully reinforcing your non-verbals.

4. Reflect back to the person what you are sensing: "This seems really important/difficult/painful to you." This helps you to connect with them on an emotional level and communicates that you are listening and understanding.

5. Carefully express what you are sensing in terms of their feelings: "I'm sensing that you're feeling frustrated...worried...anxious..." Be careful to not make a pronouncement, but rather an offering: "I am sensing...It seems like..." This kind of response invites them to clarify or expand.

6. Ask feeling questions: "What are you feeling? ...How did that make you feel?" This helps the speaker to get in touch with their heart.

7. Acknowledge the person's struggles and feelings: "You are going through so much. This is so difficult." These statements can be a huge gift, in that you are naming their struggle, one that they may be seeking to minimize or feel they should not be experiencing as so difficult.

8. If they are sharing honestly, affirm their willingness to do so: "I admire your honesty." This affirmation may be necessary if they are going to continue to be honest and express their feelings to God.

9. Invite the person to define what they mean by the words they are sharing, especially in relation to feelings. This invites deeper exploration. What does your anger, frustration, sadness feel like?

10. Refrain from judging, either through your words and non-verbals or even internally.

11. Create space with silence. Do not quickly follow their answer by asking another question or giving a response. More often than not this leads to further sharing. Your silence creates space for the other to continue to process and can lead to deeper awareness.

EIGHT CAUTIONS

The following types of comments can quickly derail or shut down honest communications:

1. Minimizing—"It could have been worse."

2. Rescuing—"You are going to be okay, so there is no need to dwell there."

3. Preaching—"God is good and will bring good out of this."

4. Dismissing—"You don't really mean that."

5. Disapproval/correcting—"You shouldn't say that, feel that, talk like that."

6. Interrupting—Jumping in, filling the silence.

7. Assuming you know what a person will say or what they mean. If you "know" what the person will say, you stop paying close attention.

8. Fixing the situation—this stops you from listening and instead occupies your mind with seeking solutions.

TYPES OF QUESTIONS

Good Questions:

- are open-ended questions, as opposed to yes/no questions.
- cause one to reflect, ponder, explore; get in touch with self, God, feelings.
- focus attention on feelings, help a person explore their heart.
- invite raw honesty and unhindered exploration of God and self.

Bad Questions:

- are closed-ended questions, requiring only a yes or no answer.

- move the person from heart to head—"what are you thinking?" (instead of feeling), asking a why question.

- are born of curiosity. This type of question is more about you.

- are questions asked too quickly without giving the person answering proper time for reflection.

- flow from your own discomfort and/or desire to control, fix, correct.

This ministry of presence creates a safe, caring place, where a person can share from the heart while you listen to what is said or not said. Yours is not an easy task, but with practice and God's help, you will be a channel of God's love, grace, patience and care. It may or may not involve asking questions, but essentially is a being with, a choosing to enter the now of the grieving person's experience and staying there. It could be a wordless walk, a sitting in the same room looking out the window together…It is you being there as a caring, non-anxious presence, devoid of an overt agenda other than to be present to God, to yourself and to the grieving person. You may feel a temptation to believe you must do more than be present, but resist that, and instead remember that both Jesus and Paul acknowledged the importance of companions in difficult times. The ministry of presence is a very important way to provide comfort for someone who is hurting.

REFLECTION

Which of the skills listed in the chapter above (pages 131–132) do you see as strengths, and which one(s) might you need to develop more fully?

Which of those cautions listed above (page 132) might be something you are prone to do and will need to intentionally avoid? Think about why that tendency seems normal to you. What's behind it?

What is a brief definition of a good question? What is a brief definition of a bad question? As you reflect on the ingredients that comprise a bad question, which one might you struggle with not doing? Why?

 A Word About Forgiveness

Forgiveness will likely be a part of the grieving journey. It begins with a desire that, if expressed, is something to be celebrated. The process is often a long one, not to be rushed, but supported.

The loss of a loved one may prompt a need to first forgive oneself before extending forgiveness to others—doctors, driver, killer, police officials, family members, even the one who died—and eventually God (see pages 76–77). Know that going in. Your place is to be an encouraging, patient presence, there to listen and support the free expression of the feelings as they surface.

CHAPTER THIRTEEN

WHAT TO SAY

In the previous chapter, we looked at the ministry of presence and how to journey with another person in their grief. In this chapter, we will hone in on the initial interaction—that first time you see a person following their loss. These initial encounters can feel very weighty and they are important, for these conversations can help foster an openness in the grieving person to have others journey with them or these conversations can push them toward isolation and withdrawal. Now the solution is not to stay away, which often is the choice of people who perceive the magnitude of the loss and the encounter, for that can cause great pain and the feeling of being deserted, ignored, dismissed. Instead, we need to come alongside the hurting person.

Yet we seldom know just the right words when we first encounter someone who has recently suffered a loss. We may feel an internal pressure to say something meaningful, something that might help the healing. Christians seem to want to share the perfect verse or pray an appropriate prayer without considering the absurdity of "appropriateness." They hope their words will help make things right, explain away the pain, but the reality is that well-meaning words often result in much additional hurt for those who are grieving.

The suggestions below won't fix anything, but they will help someone know they are not suffering alone. And, since your comments acknowledge their difficult situation, they may encourage more honesty both with self and with God. Such acknowledgement is an enormous gift in itself, and the ensuing honesty is a step closer to healing. Whenever you are conversing with someone who is grieving, try to refrain from comments that minimize or spiritualize their situation. When lost for words, practice being with the person in silence—letting your presence communicate beyond words your love and care.

The following flows from my own experiences and from the experiences of others, who I asked to tell me what was helpful to hear when they had suffered loss. As you read through the list, pay attention to the themes regarding what kinds of things are shared and what kind of things are not shared. The following suggestions can be used in face-to-face encounters, notes, cards, texts and more.

- "I am sorry for your loss."
- "I'm so sorry for all you (and your family) are going through."
- "I cannot imagine what you (and your family) are going through." This is true even if you have suffered a similar loss, as each journey with grief is different.
- "I am so sorry. I miss her/him," only if you knew the person who died.
- Share memories about the person. "I will always remember the way…" This can cause a wonderful release of pent-up emotions, so be ready for welcome tears to flow.
- "I love you and am here for you." This sentiment assumes a prior close relationship. Do not over-promise and under-deliver.
- "I am so sorry. You (and your family) are in my thoughts and prayers."
- Offer a hug in the place of words, if appropriate.

Did you notice that there are no Bible verses in these responses? How do you feel about this? This omission struck me too when I first read the list, but as I reflected on it, I felt that Bible verses can serve to minimize, rescue and bring premature comfort to one who has recently suffered loss. Down the road you may ask, "Is there a verse or passage of scripture that you find helpful at this time?"—and be prepared for an answer of no. If the person is aware you have suffered a similar loss, they may ask if there was a passage that meant a lot to you. Please be honest even if the answer is no. If you do have a passage to share, be sure to include why it meant so much to you at the time.

There may be a time when you are asked to share a passage of scripture or to read from the Bible. Be ready. Take a look at the passages referenced on page 118ff, and decide which of them feels true to your experience of God. Also note the verses best to avoid on pages 118–119.

REFLECTION

Imagine you are encountering a person you know for the first time following their loss. What is it that you desire to communicate to the person? Why?

According to this chapter, why is what you initially say to a person who has suffered loss so important?

🕮 Use the Phone

In a day and age when we do not tend to use the phone this can be a powerful means of communicating love and care for a grieving person. The person can choose to pick up or not, but if they do not, then make sure you leave a thoughtful voicemail expressing your heart for them. A friend shared with me how a message left on their phone by a friend, following a painful loss, was a source of comfort during their journey with grief. The empathy in the tone of the voice, the love and compassion expressed through the carefully chosen words shared, was something my friend went back to time and again.

Chapter Fourteen

What NOT to Say

Words have the power to bring healing or wreak destruction. When coming alongside one who is grieving, I implore you to speak with caution and thoughtfulness. The writer of Proverbs reminds us of the destructive power of words, saying, "There is one who speaks rashly like the thrusts of a sword" (Proverbs 12:18a, NASB).

I think the image of a sword-thrust is particularly poignant. Saying, "I'm sorry," after plunging a sword into someone's heart does not remove the pain or wounding caused by the sword. Keep this illustration in mind when choosing your words of "comfort and counsel." The following collection of sword-thrusts are to be avoided—well-meaning or not, they inflict injury to those already wounded. The following were gleaned from my own experiences, and from other's.

As you read through this list, spend some time pondering why each particular phrase might be hurtful. That certainly was not the intent of the well-meaning individual who shared it, but it was the result—sword-thrusts into an already hurting heart.

- "He's in a better place."
- "She's better off."
- "God needed another angel."
- "God must have wanted/needed him in Heaven."
- "Everything happens for a reason."
- "God has a plan."
- "God needed him more than you do."
- "At least you had ____ years with her."
- "It gets easier."

- "You'll move on."
- "Nathan would not want you to be sad."
- "You are choosing this pain, choosing not to be comforted."
- "You need to be strong for others, for each other, for your kids."
- "You need to be a good witness."
- "God will bring so much good out of this."
- "It is time for you to move on and get back to life."
- "Don't cry."
- "Time heals all wounds." (This statement is blatantly false, as only eternity heals all wounds. We carry the wounds of this world with us as portals into the lives of others. They become channels through which love and grace freely flow.)
- "It will be okay."
- "Death is a part of life."
- "Some things are just not meant to be."
- "At least you have another child."
- "At least you know you can become pregnant."
- "It is time you got over this."
- "You are not trusting God."
- "I know what you are feeling."
- "Why can't you get past this?"
- "Are you still grieving?"
- "God doesn't want you to be sad."
- "Just give it to God."
- "What can I do for you?" (See page 143.)
- "God doesn't give you more than you can handle."
- "Your mother/father lived a long life." (This may be true, but it doesn't lessen the emotional impact of death.)

The seeds for the following two poems were planted by my wife's and my interactions with well-meaning individuals. May our experience be a reminder of the destructive power of words and the need to choose our words carefully. When in doubt, choose silence.

Jackasses

I'm surrounded by jackasses who continually bray:
>*"He is in heaven."*
>*"It's time to move on."*
>*"Where is your faith?"*
>*"This is God's plan."*
>*"Get over it."*
>*"Don't you trust God?"*
>*"He's gone to a better place."*

God deliver me from these beasts of burden!
Their words crush me!
They arise from ignorance of you
and ignorance of me.

O God, in your grace and mercy,
smack them over the head with a two-by-four!

Our words are important and, like thrusts of a sword, our prayers can inflict pain and damage. The opportunity to pray with and for a grieving person is a treasured privilege and is not to be entered into lightly. Carefully choose your words with the Spirit's guidance, avoiding the above phrases and sentiments while owning your own tendency to fix, rescue, preach, minimize, defend God… sadly I have experienced the pain of being prayed for by others.

Prayer

I cringe when someone asks to pray for me.
I know a sermon is coming—
an avalanche of insipid Christian clichés
will soon bury me.
It's almost too much to endure
It brings no comfort
merely disgust.

REFLECTION

Take some time to reflect on the statements above, asking yourself why each might be hurtful. What might have been the motivation behind each statement?

When you speak to someone who has lost a loved one, what are you hoping to communicate, trying to accomplish? Why?

Being with One in Grief

The heart of a grieving person is raw, not always able to receive even well-intentioned words. With that in mind, I want to offer some helpful suggestions for your safe participation in the challenging process of journeying with another person in their grief. Please review and internalize these reminders before you enter into the grief of another.

- Be grounded in and dependent on the power and presence of God's love, grace, wisdom and faithfulness. God's presence with you gives you the ability to be present with another in a loving, caring and gracious way.
- Be a compassionate presence, willing to suffer with and not rescue.
- Be stingy with words meant to comfort and soothe. Express your sorrow and listen for clues as to what might be helpful during this time.
- Give the grieving person freedom to be where they are, feel what they are feeling, say what they need to say.
- Resist the temptation to defend God.
- When unsure of what to say, say nothing.
- Receive tears as a gift; affirm the willingness to be vulnerable in your presence, assuring them no apologies are necessary.
- Trust God and trust the process. God is unquestionably at work in the circumstances, but remember God "writes straight using crooked lines." The process may not play out the way you think it should.
- Pray before you go, both for the person you are visiting and for yourself. Be confident God goes before you and with you. God is at work!

CHAPTER FIFTEEN

CARING FROM A DISTANCE

Christians can feel duty-bound to physically come alongside someone who has recently suffered a loss. While this thinking may be admirable, the truth is that not everyone is wired for such duty. It's also possible they don't have a sufficiently intimate relationship with the person and would not be considered safe. It is important to know how you can best provide support: face-to-face or from a distance; both are needed!

Someone recently shared a helpful insight regarding the admittance of others into the grief process. She used the analogy of one's home: we have a front lawn, a porch, a sitting area, a kitchen table, and a bedroom. Not everyone is invited or given access to every area; it is important to understand to which area you have been given access and, more importantly, how can you best love and serve the person from there?

✄ Do Not Assume

Please do not assume that the grieving person has plenty of people attending/caring/reaching out to them. It is easy to let this assumption keep us from reaching out to those who are suffering especially since it can be a difficult thing to do in the first place. If you know the person grieving, please reach out in some tangible way (see below) that God may very well use to help the person feel seen and cared for/about rather than abandoned.

My wife and I were helped immensely by many who loved us from afar; their caring actions reminded us of God's goodness and were a healing balm to our broken hearts. Prayer is a powerful way to begin. As you lovingly hold another before God, you may be inspired to love in one of the many practical ways listed:

- Memorial or funeral help—As we were planning the memorial service for Nathan, people helped with the video, provided food for the reception, set up at the church. Someone even photographed guests at the service and assembled a precious album for us to look through and enjoy at a later time.

- Communicate information about the memorial service or other gatherings—making phone calls, sending emails, posting on Facebook.

- Attend the viewing, memorial service, or funeral, if the service is public.

- Send a plant instead of cut flowers.

- Offer your home to out-of-town family or pick them up at the airport.

- Offer to drive guests to and from the service.

- Send cards with a simple, caring message. (See the list of what not to include on pages 138-139.)

- Calling and leaving a thoughtful voicemail. The message left can continue to bring comfort to the person throughout their journey. Hearing the voice of someone who loves us can be quite powerful.

- Share stories about the deceased. Thoughtful memories and stories, written down, can be an ongoing source of comfort.

- Send a blooming plant rather than cut flowers, as flowers don't last. Disposing of dead flowers after the funeral is a painful reminder.

- Brief texts—"thinking of you," "praying for you" (see pages 135-136 regarding what to say and pages 138-139 what not to say).

- Food—provide finger food, sandwiches, vegetables and fruit—foods that are easily grabbed.

- Run errands—offer to get groceries, do shopping, stop at the cleaners.

- Organize meals—every other day is usually more than sufficient.

- Call from the grocery store to find out if they need anything. (Going out, even to the grocery store, can be surprising difficult. Facing people and answering simple questions is often unsettling.)

- Bring a cup of coffee, whether you stay or not. A friend brought coffee almost every Sunday for several weeks on the way to church, a gift beyond measure. It may be why I still drink coffee today.

- With prior permission, hire a massage therapist to come to the house. My wife loved this gift.
- Walk the dog.
- Clean the litter box.
- Care for the children, which is good for both the children and the adults.
- Pick up the kids from school.
- Arrange to have the house cleaned.
- Fill the car with gas and get it washed.
- Give gift cards for carry-out restaurants so they have a choice to eat in or take out.
- Give gift cards to movies, theme parks, or tickets to a concert, providing a welcome change of scenery.
- Offer to help with thank-you cards.
- Money can be a practical expression of love, helping to relieve some of the financial burden of travel, funeral expenses, etc. Sudden loss can mean sudden financial demands.
- Stay in touch, continue to reach out, and do not be offended if your offer to help is turned down. Next time they may respond differently. Offering help is a message of love, care and support in and of itself.

The above is not an exhaustive list, but I hope it will provide a starting point for you to demonstrate practical love. In 1 John 3:18, the Apostle John reminds us that we are to love in deed and truth. The above suggestions certainly express love and care in very practical ways.

Helping those who are hurting in these tangible ways allows those journeying with them to focus on the ministry of presence in a more intentional way. When caring for those who are hurting, we need both the ministry of the practical, as well as the ministry of presence. Both are used by God to communicate love, care and compassion. Loving from a distance is critically important in the weeks and months following a loss.

Finally, if you are given access to care from a closer proximity, perhaps you might want to offer some more personal gestures:

- Sit down with them and create a "What can I do for you?" list—a list they can draw from when someone asks, "What do you need?" This can be an enormous help and something they would likely be unable to do on their own; grief is inherently a source of confusion and causes an inability to focus (see page 17).

- Offer (with great sensitivity) to help with sorting and disposing of clothing, papers, personal items.

- Load or unload the dishwasher. Do other simple household chores that may be left undone otherwise.

- Dispose of the dead flowers.

The Parade

Within a day the parade begins:
Each participant dressed in glory and splendor
beyond compare.
Breathtaking colors and
beautiful aromas fill the senses.
They come and they come
filling room after room
with their glorious presence
but they are dying.

Each day they droop and wilt
Their beauty fades.
Their fragrance becomes a stench.

In tears, I carry each arrangement to the trash.
The parade of life and beauty
becomes a funeral procession.

The grass withers and the flowers fade
each a reminder of
the dying
the fading
of my flower
Nathan.

REFLECTION

Why is caring from a distance so very important and needed?

Why might caring from a distance not feel as important or significant as physically being with the person who is grieving?

What additional practical ways of caring (for an individual or a family) might you add to this list?

CHAPTER SIXTEEN

THE LONG HAUL

I believe people who are grieving most need support and care in the weeks and months after the funeral. Although it's helpful, of course, for friends and family to surround the survivors in the immediacy of death, a week or two later the crowds are gone. All have returned to their normal lives; their world continues as it was. But it is not so for those on the journey with grief.

Those who have suffered loss may now feel the most isolated they have felt since the death, and, at the same time, they are just beginning to realize the depth of the loss. It's a perfect storm of fatigue and emotional and psychological stress, combined with an extraordinary amount of time to feel.

Studies show the first six months are most difficult, then gradually, a new normal may begin. Actually, the entire first year is a painful year of firsts—the first holidays, the first family gatherings, the first birthday, the first anniversary of the death...

This unfortunate timing calls for companions for the long haul. Staying with those who are grieving is not something we do well as a culture or as the Church. The tendency is to quickly move through the hard times into the good times, to return to normal as soon as possible. As time passes, it is easy to assume life is getting easier for those who have suffered loss, too, and to move on with one's own activities. But "normal" no longer exists for those who have lost a loved one. In truth, the journey with grief is just now beginning in earnest.

If you want to be one who intentionally stays, accompanies another for that first year and possibly beyond, the key is your calendar and lots of prayer.

Begin by knowing that at some point you will have a palpable desire to move on. This does not mean you aren't a good friend. You have already shown great concern and given much of yourself! It is normal and important for you to re-engage with your life, but unless you are intentional you will also begin to lose contact with your hurting friend. The grieving person—exhausted, lonely, overwhelmed—hasn't the strength to reach out. As more time passes, guilt can become a hindrance to reconnecting. It has been too long. I have let them down. Do not give into those voices of condemnation. Instead drop by, text, or call—see if they are up for a visit. Your offer of love may not always be welcomed, but it is a reminder that they are seen and cared about and that is something that God can powerfully make use of too!

The Gift of Perspective

It may seem to a person grieving that even over time, nothing is changing. The cloud of grief seems perpetually dark from the inside, but if you have been walking with your friend, you have the unique gift of perspective. You can remind them of areas of incremental growth they aren't able to recognize—decreasing intensity and duration of emotions; clearer thinking; less despair and an occasional trace of joy; more normal eating and sleep patterns; more willingness to engage with others. Point out these markers of progress as they will be a source of encouragement for the future.

Some changes may begin to occur as early as two or three months out, but often it is closer to six months. Pay attention.

Below are some suggestions for caring over the long haul, while continuing to live your own life:

- Continue to pray. As you bring a person before God, God will give you wisdom as to how to continue to love in practical and creative ways.

- Utilize and depend on your calendar. Put important days, birthdays and anniversaries associated with the loss on your calendar as a reminder to contact your friend. The holidays can be especially difficult. Don't be afraid to ask how the holiday was, providing an opportunity for them to share if they so choose. Commemorate the dates with a card, potted plant, or some other acknowledgment that you are remembering with them. This ongoing thoughtfulness is a tremendous gift, demonstrating love on significant dates through an extended period of grief.

- Continue to send cards, notes and texts as reminders they are not alone and their loved one is not forgotten.

- If the cause of death is associated with a fundraiser, become involved on behalf of the family. Your support for what matters to them communicates how deeply you care.

- One person shared a particularly thoughtful gesture. "When a distant friend went through a significant loss, I bought us matching bracelets and sent one to her. I wore mine for a long time to remind me to pray for her. She wore hers when she needed the comfort of knowing someone was praying."

- Sometimes you might take a drive or a walk without any expectation of conversation. Just to be with someone without the pressure of talking or responding is a precious gift.

Be creative in your thoughtfulness. All caring is treasured. Remember most people will disappear quickly after the funeral is over. Caring for the long haul is not easy, and your life will get in the way. If you sense God inviting you into this long-term love assignment, use your calendar to help you love well. Don't be discouraged by occasional interruptions...reconnect.

REFLECTION

Reflect on your circle of friends—can you think of someone who has suffered loss in the past year? Send your friend a note or text. Even if it has been a while since you've been in contact, it will be well received. Then put a reminder on your calendar for the next time.

CHAPTER SEVENTEEN

CONCLUDING THOUGHTS

Remember, each person's journey with grief is unique. Thus, it is crucial to prayerfully move into the sacred space of grieving with another, dependent upon God and bound to God's word and promises. Refer to page 118ff.

Your interaction during the first year is critical. The list of reminders below will help you as you share God's love with someone in dire need.

- People are important during the journey with grief—you are important. In addition, the person you journey with may need the help of a pastor, a therapist or grief support group. Don't be afraid to encourage them to seek professional help.

- Love is appreciated from people close by and far off. Both have a place, and both are invaluable. Close, personal care is not for everyone; practical acts also communicate love in a powerful way.

- Functional demonstrations of love from you free others to be an emotional support, unfettered by daily necessities.

- Our words can bring healing or inflict pain like thrusts of a sword; be mindful of your words.

- We must maintain healthy boundaries—self-care is important too.

- Care extends beyond the time leading up to and immediately following the funeral. Have a plan for ongoing care through the first year; use your calendar to remind you of important dates.

- You and God are doing this together. Remain grounded in God, God's person, words and promises.

- Review the passages on page 118ff, the example of Jesus on page 124ff and Foundational Knowings (page 126ff). These truths will ground you in the enough-ness of God and allow you to creatively love out of God's love for you.

- Pray for God's wisdom and leading. Each person is different; each journey with grief is different. What was helpful yesterday may not be helpful today, so ongoing dependence on God is critical.

- Take care of you. Caring for someone, up close or from a distance, takes a toll, so make sure you are caring for yourself. Get your rest, eat well, exercise—do what you need to do to stay healthy for the journey.

- Remember, God is at work. God's love and grace abound in even the circumstances of death. We have this hope as an anchor!

REFLECTION

Reflecting on the list of reminders above, what three reminders do you feel are most important for you to keep in mind as you journey with another? Why those three? Which three reminders might you struggle with implementing as you journey with another? Why?

Use the space below to make note of any information about grief that's new to you or insights you feel may be important to keep in mind. You never know when you will be called upon to speak into the life of someone about whom you care deeply.

Epilogue

I am writing this almost fifteen years since the death of Nathan. I have not yet crossed that place in time when the years without my son outnumber the years with him, but that milestone isn't far off. As I look back over these fifteen years, much has changed. Our family moved to a new house in a new city; my wife went back to school to finish her degree; we now have two daughters-in-law, a son-in-law and five grandchildren; I started a non-profit organization and have written four books. I am more in love with my wife today than ever before, and I can honestly say that life is good. I know and experience joy, happiness and delight, which I would not have thought possible during that first excruciating year of grief. Don't misunderstand me—life has not returned to normal; rather, I have discovered a new normal. There is no going back to what was, and that has been and continues to be an adjustment. But I have learned to embrace the life I now have—a life colored by sorrow and loss, as well as by love, joy, hope and blessings.

As I reflect on what I have learned over these fifteen years, a number of things come to mind regarding my view of God, myself and others, which I will explore below.

God

The following words of Job speak to my particular situation, "Surely I spoke of things I did not understand, things too wonderful for me to know...My ears had heard of you but now my eyes have seen you" (42:3b, 5). I have come to know God as greater and grander than I ever imagined.

As I prepared for this book and read through the 300-plus poems that emerged during that first year following Nathan's death, I rediscovered the patient and relentless grace, goodness and love of God. I have come to refer to God as the ever-changing/unchanging/knowable/unknowable one. I have learned and become comfortable with God being God and not some mental or theological construct that can only hint at the real, ineffable-indescribable-inexpressible God.

I continue to learn more and more about who God is and who God is not. God is no longer in a box of my making, or the making of systematic theologians— God is free, wild, untamed and so very, very good. It can be a bit disconcerting to let God be God, but it is also awe-inspiring, faith-enriching and extremely grounding.

> *God, help me to let you continue to be God; mystery known yet unknown; infinite Love; one who loves me, likes me and loves loving me. Help me to fight the urges to cage you, control you, make you in my image.*

In light of this new sense of who God is, I have come to greatly appreciate and trust the transforming love of God in which we are rooted and grounded. God is love, and as such, loves me and loves loving me with a love I am invited to know, rely on and live life sustained and empowered by. I believe in the transforming and reconciling power of God and so believe that love wins—nothing can or will defeat God's love. I actually do not know fully what this means, but I believe it is true.

I have also come to know that God's grace is present in every situation, though admittedly not always observable or discernible. I have often come to recognize this grace present in hindsight. When I combine what I have learned about God, God's love and God's grace, I have come to the point of being able to trust God and to trust the process—to give God the benefit of the doubt when the circumstances may be screaming a very different message.

Along those lines, I have come to believe that nothing can or will separate me from God—nothing I have done, nothing that I will do, nothing that has been done to me—that God is truly and profoundly with me, and may never be closer than when I feel God's absence!

MYSELF

I have come to embrace in a far more powerful way the truth that I am loved by God—not just "God loves us," but that I personally am uniquely and particularly loved by God! In fact, God loves loving me! This has long been and is even more becoming the core of my identity, freeing me to be the person God has created, called and is empowering me to be. I am freer to love and to receive love than ever before.

OTHERS

The way I see and interact with others has dramatically changed too. I still have a long way to go in loving others, but I have made progress. My heart is enlarged and more sensitive to others. I am quicker to say, "I love you;" more comfortable being with others in their pain, questions and anger; not needing to fix or give advice; able to rejoice and weep; knowing the limited value of words and the powerful gift of presence; willing and able to suffer alongside them.

I see others as a gift for whom I am grateful, a bud needing nurturing circumstances in order to open. I have discovered that everyone has a story that needs to be heard and known if I am to be a part of their life and that, sadly, most people have stories involving some degree of brokenness, dysfunction, abuse, or betrayal. Each person's life, path, perspectives, understanding and experience tend to be different from mine, often in significant ways. So I no longer assume I know others, but seek to understand, accept and meet them where they are.

Random things I have noticed and named:

- I still miss Nathan.
- I still want him back.
- I still see the effects on my wife, but they are not as pronounced, as perpetual.
- I am still hurting, but not even close to what I experienced that first year. Pain is still with me, but no longer overwhelming and debilitating.
- I am still tender when it comes to seeing pictures and viewing videos of Nathan.
- I still wonder what kind of man, son, uncle, father he would have been.
- I don't dream of him as much as I used to.
- My memories do not always lead to tears but can bring joy.
- The holidays, his birthday, the anniversary of his death, are still difficult, but also bring joy, even happiness. When we gather we are able to enjoy one another, and the atmosphere is much lighter and livelier.
- When my children, daughter-in-law or grandchildren are late, I become concerned. I find myself hoping they are okay.
- I continue to see God use this horrific event and its fruit to bring encouragement and hope to others.
- I have a greater hope in and desire for heaven.

Fifteen years later I am different, having been shaped by the death of Nathan, but I am not defined by it. I believe I am a better person today because of all I, we, have journeyed through, but I still would love to have him in my life. I still miss him and I pray that no other parents have to bury their child, yet I know that in this broken world of ours, it will happen again and again and again. But I also know we have a God who is with us, bidden or unbidden, suffering with us, weeping with us—sustaining us with divine love and grace. And so I have hope for myself and for you, as we continue to journey after the loss of a loved one. It is not, will not be easy, but there is hope now and to come in the future. Time does not heal all wounds, but eternity does when perfect Love has its way with us.

Here is a poem I penned as I was beginning to write this book. It speaks to the ongoing reality of this journey.

Again

I sit alone in a room
light streaming through
floor-to-ceiling windows
trees, hills, wispy clouds all peeking in at me
cars entering and exiting the parking lot below—
life, beauty and light all around me
reminders that I am not alone.

I am here writing about grief
an undertaking already transporting me
back to my own grief—
a time when life and beauty mocked me,
trees and hills ignored me,
dark menacing clouds filled the horizon.

fourteen years have passed and
the pain remains—today I feel the rising
tide of sorrow. I feel the draw
of distractions, the temptation to numb.
I feel myself being carried out
into a sea of despair.

I name, acknowledge and explore these
feelings but I am no longer undone by them,

my feet firmly planted in the hope and love
of God I have come to know through
my ongoing season of grief—

so I proceed in my writing,
revisiting the pain
afflicted but not crushed;
> *not despairing,*
> *not abandoned,*
> *not destroyed.*

I will follow and I will write.

ADDITIONAL RESOURCES

Broken Hallelujahs: Learning to Grieve the Big and Small Losses of Life, by Beth Allen Slevcove. This book provides a wonderful collection of real-life stories, down-to-earth exercises and the needed encouragement to feel, express and engage with grief in honest ways. Beth, drawing from her own experiences, provides practical wisdom for those journeying through their own grief and those who are invited to accompany others through grief. It deals with all types of loss.

Lament for A Son, by Nicholas Wolterstorff. This is a father's personal reflection following the death of his son. It is intensely personal, very honest and insightful. Also, at just over a hundred pages, it is not overwhelming to read and may help you put into words the very things you are experiencing as a result of your loss. I found this book very helpful early on.

A Grace Disguised: How the Soul Grows through Loss, by Jerry L. Sittser. Drawing from the tragic losses in his own life, Jerry provides practical as well as theological insight and understanding regarding suffering, loss, grief and how God can and does use such tragedies in our life to continue to grow and transform us. I found this book a bit overwhelming at first, but then extremely helpful, as I became more able to enter into and interact with the material.

The Truth about Grief: The Myth of Its Five Stages and the New Science of Loss, by Ruth Davis Konigsberg. This book takes on the myths and misunderstanding of the theory of "the stages of grief," as well as some of the practices of the grief industry, especially in America. It is a very informative and interesting read that seeks to call to account those individuals and groups that endeavor to make a living by fostering perpetual grief in people—what she calls the commercialization of grief. It also provides the current findings in the field of grief studies.

www.b-ing.org, is my website, where you may find additional poems on grief that do not appear in this book, along with a recording of the guided meditation that appears on page 84 of this book. All these resources can be found on the website, under the *Journey with Grief* tab.

WORKS CITED

Konigsberg, Ruth Davis. *The Truth About Grief* (New York: Simon & Schuster, 2011).

Lamott, Anne. *Bird by Bird: Some Instructions on Writing and Life* (New York: Anchor, 1995).

McKee, Robert. *Story: Substance, Structure, Style, and the Principles of Screenwriting.* (New York: Regan Books, 1997.)

Roe, Gary. *Heartbroken: Healing from the Loss of a Spouse.* (Wellborn: GR Healing Resources, 2015.)

Slevcove, Beth Allen. *Broken Hallelujahs: Learning to Grieve the Big and Small Losses of Life* (Downers Grove: InterVarsity Press, 2016).

Sittser, Jerry L. *A Grace Disguised: How the Soul Grows through Loss* (Grand Rapids: Zondervan, 2004).

Wolterstorff, Nicholas. *Lament For A Son* (Grand Rapids: Wm. B. Eerdmans, 1987).

About the Author

Larry Warner, who refers to himself as the beloved of God and enjoys going barefoot, is a teacher, a pastor and a spiritual director. He is an associate professor in the area of spiritual formation, Ignatian spirituality and spiritual direction, currently teaching at the Institute of Spiritual Formation at Biola University and Bethel Seminary, San Diego.

As a spiritual director, Larry meets with pastors and church leadership throughout the world. He is a retreat leader, author of *Discernment, God's Will and Living Jesus; Journey with Jesus* and co-author of *Imaginative Prayer for Youth Ministry*. In 2005 he founded b (b-ing.org), a spiritual support organization for pastors, missionaries, seminarians and church staffs, which encourages them to open to God's love and to live Jesus in new and deeper ways.

Larry has a varied vocational background. He was a youth pastor for eleven years, a Los Angeles Deputy Sheriff for six years, and a senior pastor for ten years, before founding and leading b for nearly twelve years. Though roles and experiences changed, his passion has remained the same: to help people more fully embrace God's love and to live more fully into and out of the person God has called and created them to be, free to love and serve others in life-giving ways.

Larry has been married for over 39 years; he is a father of four and a grandfather of five.

Other Books by Larry Warner

Journey with Jesus (Downers Grove: InterVarsity Press, 2010).

Discernment, God's Will and Living Jesus (Oceanside: barefooted pub, 2016).

Acknowledgements

There are many who gave me valuable input and provided timely encouragement as I was writing this book.

My wife, Donna, was a constant support, even when I disappeared into my office for long blocks of time or went away for days to write. She was and is a wonderful support and I am better for having her in my life.

Additionally, I am grateful for Andy, Blair, Amy, Laura, Alexis and Cynthia, who each took time to read portions of the book, providing valuable suggestions, insights and encouraging comments.

My editor, Jessica Snell, once again brought her grammatical prowess and editorial expertise to this project, bringing greater value to the reader. It was my hope that she would have the time to take on this project and work her magic—and she did!

Christine Smith, a talented and exceedingly creative person, is the artist who designed my cover and who, as always, was a joy to work with. She extended me grace and demonstrated patience as we moved ever closer to the final cover.

And finally, I am hugely grateful for the role Gail Steel played once again. She has become a trusted partner and friend on this writing adventure. Again she took my rough first drafts and helped make sense of my words and turned convoluted sentences and paragraphs into something intelligible—offering suggestions, reworking material and providing timely encouragement.

Thank you one and all. It truly takes a village to raise a book!

Made in the USA
San Bernardino,
CA